PGA CENTENNIAL

CELEBRATING THE HISTORY OF
THE GOLF PROFESSIONAL

Written by Billy Dettlaff, PGA

Edited by John Steinbreder

SKYBOX PRESS · SAN DIEGO

CONTENTS

OPPOSITE Argentinian José Jurado, a runner-up in the 1931 Open Championship, became a popular teacher and golf ambassador during the golden age of golf in the 1930s.

PREFACE

O n the occasion of the PGA of America's centennial, we pause to chronicle a remarkable century of growth for member professionals and the game of golf itself. As a great philosopher once said, "a small body of determined spirits fired by an unquenchable faith in their mission can alter the course of history."

On April 10, 1916, 35 charter members were among those elected to the first nationwide all-professional golf association in our country. Their faith in the mission of the PGA, and the faith of those that have followed in their footsteps, is what we are truly celebrating in this commemorative centennial book.

As the stewards of our Association 100 years later, we believe it is critically important to tell the stories of those who came before us, who boldly stepped off a ship into America to elevate the golf profession. They understood what the rite of passage means to be a golf professional. It is a passion to inspire, to teach, to mentor, to lead, and ultimately to perform on the course. *PGA Centennial: Celebrating the History of the Golf Professional* is a chronology of the individuals who have helped make golf the great game it is today as well as the nearly $70 billion business it represents in the United States.

Thanks to the tireless research and comprehensive writings of PGA Master Professional Billy Dettlaff, whose work *Doctors of the Game* is excerpted in the pages that follow, we are thrilled to share the celebration of a remarkable 100 years with you, our fellow PGA Professionals and friends in golf.

We hope you will share our enthusiasm in learning about the men and women responsible for designing and building golf courses, teaching the game, manufacturing golf equipment, managing competitions, and most of all, working tirelessly to promote the game.

Today, as it was with every PGA founder, wearing the PGA badge is a symbol of achievement and responsibility that comes with being a leader in the golf industry as well as a professional's local community. We invite you to learn more about the PGA Professional and this wonderful lineage that has continued to ensure that golf is not just a sport but a passionate and spiritual experience leading to a lifetime of friendships, exhilarating moments, and shared experiences.

The stories that follow shed light on the nuanced aspects of the game while accomplishing what those 35 charter members a century ago intended: to inspire future generations of PGA Professionals and remind us of the quintessential American dream.

Derek A. Sprague
PGA PRESIDENT

Paul K. Levy
PGA VICE PRESIDENT

Suzy Whaley
PGA SECRETARY

OPPOSITE Errie Ball, who served the PGA of America a record 83 years, gave lessons past his 100th birthday and was a 2011 inductee into the PGA Hall of Fame.

FOREWORD *by Jack Nicklaus, PGA*

As the PGA of America celebrates an enormous milestone, I find myself reminiscing about the many PGA Professionals who carried the torch for those first 100 years and how their passion for this wonderful game sparked an amazing period of growth. Many of them were descendants of hardy Scots who were the pioneers of our sport.

These PGA Professionals were multitaskers from the start: playing and teaching the game to aspiring players. They also made club-making an art and continued to experiment with the golf ball, all bidding to polish it—along with the game—like a precious gem.

Many of those early professionals ultimately boarded a ship to seek new challenges and careers in America. They became the leaders of golf in the United States, including at the PGA of America, where they inspired generations to learn the craft, teach it with care, and become the stewards of the game's future. I have been a PGA member since 1966 and am proud to be among the men and women who make it a habit to greet each new student as if we had known each other all our lives. PGA members recognize the importance of building friendships in a game that was founded on relationships.

Like the Scots of generations past, I grew up appreciating what this game offered in terms of developing one's character, the valuable life lessons it taught, the challenges it presented, and the joy it gave me each day. The journey of the golf professional, as this book chronicles, includes men and women who were mentors to so many.

One such mentor was Jack Grout, who fell in love with golf at age 8, joining the caddie corps at Oklahoma City Golf and Country Club. By age 15, he was giving lessons. He would become a Tour professional, before shaping his career as one of the finest instructors of his time. I met Jack at age 10—soon after he arrived at my home club of Scioto Country Club in Columbus, Ohio—and he shaped my career and path and enhanced my love for golf. When I first met him as a young boy, I called him Mr. Grout. As I grew, along with our relationship, he became J. Grout to me.

He also became like a second father to me, especially after my father passed in 1970. J. Grout would be my only instructor from the day I attended one of his junior golf classes at Scioto until his passing in 1989. He was never one to make himself obvious on the practice tee of a major championship or tournament, instead preferring to stay in the shadows or on the periphery. But I always knew he was there—and he was—as a friend first and a mentor second.

PGA Professionals like J. Grout are what sustain our sport. They expand the world of golf in the eyes of their students. Bob Toski, a contemporary of Jack's and a teaching legend himself, said of J. Grout, "Time will prove his greatness."

Indeed, time has been the test, a perpetual measuring stick of what golf means to its most avid followers and to the landscape of American sports culture.

The PGA of America's membership, composed of some 28,000 Professionals, grew from a strong core a century ago. They did more than just play the game well and teach it well. They weathered the tragedies of two world wars and a Great Depression on their way to building momentum to a future that presented unlimited possibilities.

From the earliest generation of golf professionals to the trained business acumen of today's PGA members, you will find, as did I, there are many exceptional individuals wearing the PGA badge. My congratulations to the men and women of the PGA of America. The PGA's centennial is to be embraced and celebrated throughout the 41 Sections. Thank you for providing the path and guidance, the same as a kind and humble teacher afforded me in my youth.

Good golfing.

OPPOSITE Jack Nicklaus, *right*, and his longtime teacher, Jack Grout, enjoyed a special bond that began when the Golden Bear was 10 and defined mentoring in golf's modern era.

INTRODUCTION

W here would we be without golf professionals?

Not content to remain in the British Isles, many Old World golf professionals traveled to America to help introduce and grow the game here. They designed and built the first courses in the States and then ran the golf operations at the clubs that were established around those layouts. Along the way, they taught a nation of golf neophytes how to play, always emphasizing the importance of doing so by the same rules that had been promulgated by the first golf societies in Scotland. Those immigrant professionals also educated Americans as to the nuances of instruction and equipment, and they organized and competed in many of the first tournaments held in the United States.

Quite understandably, those fellows dominated the American golf world at the turn of the 20th century, and as a result, they filled most of the chairs around the table at the 1916 luncheon at the Wanamaker Store in New York City that led to the founding of the PGA of America. In the months and years ahead, they also helped develop that fledgling organization as they continued to build and grow the greater game of golf in the United States. Thanks to the early efforts of the immigrant professionals, the sport prospered, and the PGA thrived.

As the PGA of America enters its second century, it stands as a leader in the golf industry and is one of the largest sports organizations in the world. Its longevity and stature give us good reason to herald the reaching of that milestone, and what better way to do that than by paying tribute to the men and women who have served the game so well and so faithfully through the years, beginning with Allan Robertson—the Scotsman who is regarded as the first true golf professional and was aided in his cramped St. Andrews cottage by a teenage apprentice named Tom Morris—and moving to the 28,000 PGA Professionals who nobly and capably serve the game today.

Much has changed about that job and the duties that Allan Robertson and Old Tom Morris performed in the early 1800s are quite a bit different from those that PGA Professionals must undertake today. However, two things have remained constants. One is a deep passion for golf and an occasionally obsessive desire to bring new people into the game and help those who already play enjoy it even more, and the other is an almost superhuman ability to excel at a multitude of tasks. Robertson and Morris could compete and caddie with the best of them as they also made and sold the finest equipment of the time and gave lessons. As for the professionals of the 21st century, they must be just as versatile and skilled, and no one has described the imperatives of the job better than Darrell Kestner, the esteemed PGA director of golf at Deepdale Golf Club outside New York City: "All you need to do is dress and run a golf shop like Ralph Lauren, play like Jack Nicklaus, teach like Jim Flick, be a nice person like the pope, and be a great storyteller and personality like Jimmy Fallon."

Ever since the Association's founding in 1916, the Professionals of the PGA of America have been meeting the many challenges of their positions, and they, and the game, have prospered as a result. The Association started with 35 charter members and an original network of 7 Sections. Today, it boasts some 28,000 members who operate out of 41 Sections nationwide. Each and every one of those men and women share a legacy with Allan Robertson and Old Tom, with the first immigrant professionals who crossed the Atlantic Ocean to bring golf to the New World, and with all the PGA of America members who followed those pioneers and helped make the game and the Association what they are today.

OPPOSITE Old Tom Morris, perhaps the most influential figure in golf history, and his prodigal son, Young Tom, won a combined eight major championships.

CHAPTER

ONE

Scottish Roots

By the time Allan Robertson was born in St. Andrews in the fall of 1815, golf had already taken hold in Scotland. In fact, the game had been played in that nation since at least the mid-15th century, and by the mid-1700s, golf societies were sprouting throughout the land, including one that would become the Royal and Ancient Golf Club of St. Andrews. Robertson's father, David, was a feathery ball maker as well as a caddie on the links there. He was also a pretty fair golfer.

Back then, the game was still a bastion for the wealthy, mainly due to the high cost of equipment. Families that crafted golf clubs and balls, like the Robertsons, were not counted among the well-to-do, but they had easier access to the sport than most working-class individuals because they possessed the necessary gear to play. As a result, the artisans and their children generally became competent golfers.

Not surprisingly, David Robertson's son Allan was drawn to the game. Golf would turn out to be much more than recreation for him, and he came to make the sport his occupation, integrating ball-making with caddying, teaching, and playing. What made him unusual was his superior talent in each of those endeavors and the fact that he could perform them all better than anyone else in Scotland. Robertson was also the first person to derive his entire livelihood from the game, which is why he is regarded as the first true golf professional and the original "doctor of the game."

Described as a "compact, robust fellow, short-necked with a black trimmed beard," Robertson lived much of his adult life in a stone cottage located on the edge of the Old Course in St. Andrews. The kitchen served as a workshop for making feathery balls and what must be regarded as the first pro shop, for he sold his wares through a window on the side of that room. Through that opening, Robertson also made arrangements with customers looking for caddies, playing partners, or teachers. Working with him in that building for a spell in the mid-1800s was a young apprentice who would come to be known as Old Tom Morris.

Robertson's skills were highly respected in Scotland, as these words from the *Chambers's Edinburgh Journal* indicate: "There is a ball maker, Allan Robertson by name, who besides having the highest character for his wares is reputed to be the best player in St. Andrews and consequently in Scotland—I may as well add, in the world. This is an eminence which golfers must admire and in the little world of the links men of estate and title will be heard speaking of worthy Allan as if he were a kind of King amongst them."

Challenge matches between the top players of that era generated great interest and early publicity for the game and helped initiate the first major explosion of golf that covered over half a century leading into the late 1880s. It also helped put money in the pockets of those who played in them—and no one was better in those competitions than Robertson.

Typically, the contests were organized in one of two manners: proposed stakes between the players themselves in open challenges often advertised in local newspapers, or by local promoters who with great pride backed their favorite professionals by posting large wagers in their favor. Early on, the very best golfers developed a stable of benefactors who were oftentimes the very same people they caddied for, and those fellows would stake the players to matches, functioning in many ways as a sort of rich man's entertainment, much like horse racing and boxing. They also served as vehicles for enhancing civic pride, as the competitions often featured men from different towns, courses, or golf societies.

While Robertson was not invincible, as some early writings suggest, it was those sorts of matches that created the demand not only for his feathery balls, but also for his services as a playing partner, teacher, and caddie for wealthy aristocrats. His playing prowess allowed him to grow his business substantially as it also enhanced his stature in the sport, and that led to opportunities in other aspects of the game, such as architecture. In fact, historians credit Robertson for supervising the widening of the Old Course in St. Andrews in the mid-1800s as

ABOVE Scottish golf professionals of distinction in the 1850s, *from left*: James Wilson, Willie Dunn, Bob Andrew, Willie Park, Old Tom Morris, Allan Robertson, and David Anderson. OPPOSITE The first prize of the Open Championship, the Challenge Belt, was retired by Young Tom Morris in 1870 following his third consecutive victory.

well as creating a new green for the fabled Road Hole there. He also laid out a 10-hole course that formed the foundation of the present Open Championship layout at Carnoustie, in Scotland.

In 1856, Robertson also came to assume the role as keeper of the green for the Royal and Ancient Golf Club of St. Andrews, receiving the annual sum of £25 to ensure that the links there were in good order. Three years later, he died, at the age of 44. His was an untimely passing, but before he had gone, he had laid the groundwork for what would become one of the most important positions in the game as he showed the next generation how to do it.

As good as Allan Robertson was as a player, teacher, and ball-maker, perhaps his greatest gift to golf was mentoring Old Tom Morris, who is among the most significant figures in the history of the game. It may have been Old Tom's father who introduced the lad to golf, but it was Robertson who educated and nurtured Morris and helped make him the game's first superstar.

Thomas Mitchell Morris was born in St. Andrews, Scotland, on June 16, 1821. His father was a weaver and part-time postman and also a proficient golfer and caddie, and his son Tom started playing the game when he was six or seven years of age. Morris's father wanted something better for son Tom than the uncertain life as a weaver, so he arranged for him to start an apprenticeship with Robertson. Morris was only 14 when he left the security of the family home to move into Robertson's cottage and begin working there, his room and board his only compensation.

The year was 1835, and Robertson was just beginning his 25-year run as the greatest competitive golfer of his era. He was also regarded as one of the best ball-makers in the world, and that meant it could not have been a better time for Morris to be taken under Robertson's tutelage. As he taught Morris about ball-making, Robertson also brought Morris along as a player. In time, they started competing

as partners, often against the best professionals in the game and frequently coming out on top, but then an accidental yet difficult philosophical break took place.

The growing popularity of the gutta-percha ball caused great concern to the elder Robertson, and he feared the cheaper, easily manufactured implement would end his feathery business. So, he sought to use both his and Morris's respected reputations to fight the popularity of the new ball and proposed that they never endorse nor even play with the cheap substitute. Sometime later, Morris was on the Old Course when he ran out of his own inventory of featheries and accepted the offer from his partner to use a gutta-percha instead. Morris admitted that he "took to it at once, and as we were playing in, it so happened that we met Allan Robertson coming out, and someone told him I was playing a very good game with one of the new gutta balls." Morris related that when they later met in his shop, "we had some high words

about the matter, and it was then and there we parted company."

After that falling out, Morris set up his own shop in St. Andrews and is believed to have made both feathery and gutta-percha balls during these transition years. He may also have entered into the club-making trade in some manner. His new business has been dated to 1848, and while he and Robertson never worked together again, they remained friends and frequent playing partners until Robertson's death.

Morris stayed in St Andrews as an independent for a total of three years until he accepted the newly created position of keeper of the green at Prestwick in 1851. Among his first duties there was improving the informal, makeshift links, and soon a new 12-hole course began to take shape.

As was the case with his mentor, Morris had expanded into the world of course architecture and maintenance, and under his guidance, Prestwick became the first prominent course in that part of Scotland.

OPPOSITE English-born Willie Dunn Jr. became a respected golf course designer and opened the first professional golf shop in the United States. ABOVE Golf stars of 1889: C. Gibson, R. Simpson, Sgt. Major Bosworth, J. Hutchings, J. Longhurst, G. Alexander, D. Grant, J. Allan, A. Kirkaldy, J. H. Taylor, G. Cawsey, D. Rolland, A. Simpson, W. Hutchings, David Anderson, H. Kirkaldy, P. Paxton, D. Brown, Tom Morris Sr., J. Burns, T. Kirk, J. Kirkaldy, B. Sayers, D. Aytone, J. Kay, and F. Hearn.

IN MEMORY OF

ALLAN ROBERTSON

WHO DIED 1ST SEPT 1859

The passing of Allan Robertson in 1859 had created a huge void in the small world of competitive golf, and that prompted a group of Prestwick members to come up with the novel idea of staging an event for the best professionals in the game. Concerned with the possible problems of opening the tournament up to all comers and drawing a group of uncouth, objectionable caddies in conjunction with the top professionals to their tourney, the organizers sent invitations to the secretaries of eleven of the 35 clubs in existence at the time. The secretaries were advised to wisely select their best two professionals, keeping appropriate character in mind, as they would be representing their home clubs. The event would be a one-day affair played over 36 holes, that being three times around the 12-hole Prestwick course, and club members commissioned the manufacture of a £25 Moroccan red leather belt adorned with silver medallions that would serve as the championship trophy. There would be no prize money.

So, on a windy Wednesday, October 17, 1860, eight "crack" players teed it up in what would later become known as the Open Championship. As host professional, Morris was given the honor of hitting the first tee shot, and at 11:30 that morning, he ushered in the era of stroke play championships. He ended up finishing second, by 2 shots, to Willie Park Sr. of Musselburgh, Scotland.

The following year, the club decided to include amateurs, and the 1861 field more than doubled, to 18 participants. This time, Morris turned the tables on Park, beating him by 4 strokes for the title. A year later, Morris successfully defended, and then won again in 1864.

The following year marked the first time a father and son played in the same Open Championship, as Morris brought along his 14-year-old son, Thomas Mitchell Morris Jr. In addition, the tournament likely marked the first time that golfers began to distinguish the father and son as "Old Tom" and "Young Tom."

Old Tom did not fare well in the 1865 edition of the Open Championship and came up just short the following year, finishing fourth, but he triumphed once again in 1867, taking his fourth and final Open. Young Tom was 5 shots back in fourth place, signaling at age 16 that he was ready to compete with the finest golfers in the land.

The next year, Young Tom demonstrated that he was the best, capturing what would be the first of three consecutive Open Championships and retiring the Challenge Belt in the process. With that prize no longer available, organizers did not hold the Open in 1871, but they staged it again a year later, with Young Tom showing that he had not lost his dominating talent. He emerged victorious, and his name became the first to be etched onto the new champion's trophy, the Claret Jug.

In early September 1875, right after he had played in a tournament at nearby North Berwick, Young Tom Morris received a telegram requesting that he return immediately to St. Andrews because his wife of only one year was gravely ill and in childbirth. By the time he arrived, both his wife and infant son had passed.

A little over four months later, on Christmas Day in 1874, Young Tom died suddenly. He was only 24 years old, and many attributed his passing to a broken heart.

With four consecutive Open victories, Young Tom left behind a competitive playing record that has never been matched, and in his far-too-short life, he had also established a new professional definition in the game. He never served as a caddie or was formally attached to a club as a keeper of the green or professional. Rather, Young Tom made his living solely as a player, competing in tournaments and exhibition matches. That made him the first of another golfing breed, that of touring professional.

By the time Young Tom died, Old Tom Morris had moved back to St. Andrews to take up his appointment as the first salaried professional to the Royal and Ancient Golf Club as well as keeper of the green. His staff for the latter position consisted of one man who could help him two days a week, and his equipment inventory was one wheelbarrow, one spade, and one shovel.

Old Tom proved to be just as adept as a keeper of the green as he was a player and club professional, and he is credited with making multiple contributions to the realm of golf course agronomy in that role. Among them was the concept of topdressing both greens and fairways, the regular filling of fairway divots, the separation of the teeing ground from the putting surfaces, and the need to address natural drainage and irrigation issues.

Upon his return to St. Andrews, Old Tom set up a more formal club-making operation in a new shop just off the 18th green of the Old Course, and it did very well, thanks to a name and reputation he had built over the years. Morris had become a golf celebrity, and golfers seeking access to the Old Course or an assignment of a caddie came by his shop to finalize arrangements. Even those who did not plan to play sought the opportunity to say hello to the famous champion, and Old Tom reciprocated gladly. He was a noted storyteller, and small crowds gathered in front of his shop to hear tales of early golf matches and how Young Tom

captured the Open's championship belt with his three consecutive victories.

Over the decades, Old Tom also developed a noted reputation for designing new courses and upgrading existing layouts. All told, he is credited with laying out 69 tracks, among them such masterpieces as Royal North Devon, Muirfield, Royal County Down, Royal Portrush, and the New Course at St. Andrews. He also made additions and revisions to the original Allan Robertson—designed Championship Course at Carnoustie, the Old Course in St. Andrews, Royal Dornoch, and, of course, Prestwick.

Perhaps it was a combination of Old Tom and the town in which he lived that did so much for the advancement of the golf professional's position and, in turn, the game. He linked a great playing record, a superior club- and ball-making business, a keen eye for course design, and a visionary understanding of golf course maintenance concepts with a likeable personality that drew respect from individuals from every social level. Those traits combined with his St. Andrews location showcased him and the game to the thousands of golfers who came to the "Auld Grey Toon" to play its courses.

To his honor, when the original Professional Golfer Association was created in Great Britain in February of 1902, its founders elected Old Tom honorary vice captain and saluted him as "a man of unspoiled simplicity and genuineness of character."

Old Tom Morris died just a few weeks before his 87th birthday, from a fall down a flight of stairs in the New Golf Club in St. Andrews, not far from the 18th tee of the Old Course. He was buried by the east wall of the cemetery at the St. Andrews Cathedral, next to the grave of his beloved son, Young Tom.

OPPOSITE The gravestone of Young Tom Morris, buried near his wife and son at St. Andrews Cathedral Burial Ground.

IN MEMORY OF
"TOMMY"
SON OF THOMAS MORRIS
WHO DIED 25TH DECEMBER 1875 AGED 24 YEARS

DEEPLY REGRETTED BY NUMEROUS FRIENDS AND ALL GOLFERS
HE THRICE IN SUCCESSION WON THE CHAMPION'S BELT
AND HELD IT WITHOUT RIVALRY AND YET WITHOUT ENVY
HIS MANY AMIABLE QUALITIES
BEING NO LESS ACKNOWLEDGED THAN HIS GOLFING ACHIEVEMENTS

THIS MONUMENT HAS BEEN ERECTED
BY CONTRIBUTIONS FROM SIXTY GOLFING SOCIETIES

CHAPTER

TWO

Immigrants to America

L ike the down and seed of thistles floating with the wind, adventurous Scotsmen began carrying their beloved game to the New World in the latter part of the 1800s. Golf was starting to take hold in North America at that time, and the first clubs were being formed. The immigrant golf professionals were filling a growing need for leadership and experience at those places.

There was the Royal Montreal Golf Club in the Canadian province of Quebec, which came into being in 1873 and is regarded today as the oldest, continuously played golf club on the continent. Some years later, a transplanted Scot named John Reid, who was living in the suburbs of New York City, asked a friend to purchase some golf balls and a set of clubs on a visit to Great Britain. The man obliged, traveling to Old Tom Morris's Golf Shop in St. Andrews to make the acquisition. Once he received those goods, Reid laid out a makeshift course consisting of three holes on his property. It was there, on an early spring day in 1888, that he played his first round of golf in America. That summer, Reid expanded the course to six holes, and then he organized what is now recognized as the oldest golf club in continual operation in the United States, the Saint Andrews Golf Club.

The royal and ancient game also began to blossom in the Chicago area, thanks to Charles Blair Macdonald. A native of Niagara Falls, Ontario, who grew up in the Windy City, he had first learned and played the game as a student at St. Andrews University, under the tutelage of Old Tom, and is often called the Father of Golf in America. Macdonald and a few friends built a 9-hole layout in Belmont, Illinois, in 1892. Two years later, Macdonald led a group that purchased 200 acres in nearby Wheaton, and thus the Chicago Golf Club was born, with the new course being laid by Macdonald. Many of the holes were renditions of classics designs from British Isles tracks, and the track today is recognized as the first 18-hole course in America.

In 1889, Scotsman Willie Dunn Jr., from the famous golfing Dunn family of Musselburgh, was designing a course at Biarritz, France, when three wealthy vacationing Americans approached him, among them W. K. Vanderbilt. They were captivated by the game, and when they returned to the States, they built a 12-hole layout near their East End Long Island summer homes, hiring the Royal Montreal professional W. F. Davis to handle the design. They dubbed their new association the Shinnecock Hills Golf Club.

Slightly to the northeast, a group of Rhode Islanders formed the Newport Golf Club. They, too, hired Davis to create the design, and he built a nine holes on a piece of land called Brenton Point in 1892.

During this same time, a little further north near Boston, the executive committee of The Country Club in Brookline, Massachusetts, decided to add golf to a roster of activities that included archery, horse racing, and shooting. Six holes opened in March of 1893. The following year, club leaders replaced the original course with a 9-hole design by Scotsman Willie Campbell, who would go on to become their first golf professional.

The American game was quickly expanding in 1894, yet it lacked any form of ruling body or recognized championship. During that year, Shinnecock Hills, Newport, and Saint Andrews each held events with the purpose of identifying a national amateur champion. Fearing the eventual failure of the game in the United States without a recognized governing body, delegates from those three retreats as well as The Country Club in Brookline met to discuss the establishment of an American ruling body for golf. A year later, the United States Golf Association (USGA) was born.

That autumn, in 1895, the USGA staged its first U.S. Amateur, which was played at Newport and won by Charles Blair Macdonald. The next day the first U.S. Open followed, on the same track, with the club's 19-year-old assistant professional Horace Rawlins coming out on top.

Three years later, the USGA made what was perhaps an even more important move when it decided to adopt the Rules of the Royal and Ancient Golf Club of St. Andrews. That ballot affirmed that golf in the United States would be played as it was in the British Isles.

Though golf was very much in its infancy by the end of the 19th century, it was clear that the game was slowly but surely catching the fancy of the sporting populace of the United States. According to *Harper's Official Golf Guide*, 982 courses were operating across the land at that time. That roster included 90 18-hole layouts, 715 9-holers, and 66 tracks comprised of six holes each. In addition, there were 111 courses with no designated number of holes.

The development of golf in America provided multiple business opportunities, and several of the best professionals from the British Isles crossed the Atlantic to pursue them. The first came with a pioneering courage and a desire not only to nurture their own personal prosperity but also to help build the game they loved in the United States. Theirs was a fortuitous arrival for golf enthusiasts in the States, as the Scots were able to supply the expertise that was needed if the fledgling American game was to flourish. In fact, the early immigrant professionals were in such demand that they changed jobs frequently, moving from place to place as different clubs recruited them.

One such person was Willie Davis. A native of Carnoustie, Scotland, he became the first working golf professional in North America when he took a job at Royal Montreal in 1881. A decade later, he accepted a commission to lay out the original Shinnecock Hills course. The following year, in 1892, he built a 9-hole track at the Newport Golf Club in Rhode Island, and in 1893 he became its professional. Davis worked at that retreat for the next several years, building interest in the game among members of that young club and playing head-to-head matches against fellow Scottish professionals, like Willie Dunn Jr. and Willie Campbell, that served to generate some extra cash for the players as they also promoted the game. In time, Davis

moved to the Apawamis Club in Westchester County, New York, where he was employed until his death in 1902.

The son of a noted player and club-maker from Musselburgh, Scotland, Willie Dunn began working in the game when he was a wee lad of 13, apprenticing at the North Berwick Golf Club in East Lothian for his older brother Tom, who was the professional there. In 1886, Dunn the younger accepted an invitation to construct a course for the Royal North Devon Golf Club in England. Three years later, he helped build a track in Biarritz, France, where an elegant resort

had been established. It was there that Dunn met a trio of vacationing American industrialists who became enthralled with the potential of golf in America after watching the Scotsman play an exhibition.

Upon their return to the States, those businessman set about founding the Shinnecock Hills Golf Club in Southampton, New York. Two years after it had opened, they asked Dunn to be their seasonal professional, acting as instructor and ball- and club-maker. He served in that position from 1893 through 1895. While holding that job, Dunn opened what is regarded

ABOVE Scottish immigrants Alex Smith, *center*, the 1906 and 1910 U.S. Open Champion, and James Maiden, *far right*, formed the golf staff at Nassau Country Club in Glen Cove, New York, at the turn of the Twentieth Century. Maiden, a member of the organizing committee of the PGA of America in 1916, is credited with brother, Stewart, in inspiring the golf swing of Bobby Jones.

as the first golf professional shop in the United States, selling from that place of business the implements he made.

Dunn also relied on competitive exhibition matches to support his new life in America, and he played in many of the first ones ever held in the United States. Oftentimes, his opponents included Willie Campbell and W. F. "Willie" Davis. These pioneer professionals came to be known as the "Three Willies," and another visiting Scottish professional, Willie Park Jr., joined them on occasion.

In time, Dunn began designing golf courses, such as the Ardsley Casino course (now the Ardsley Country Club) in New York. He also opened the country's first off-course retail golf shop, in New York City. Dunn's new business target was the growing force of American golfers, including those in that metropolis who were beginning to play the new Van Cortlandt Park Golf Course, which was founded in the Bronx. It was America's first public course.

In addition, Dunn got involved with the mass production of golf clubs, working first for the Bridgeport Gun Implement Company based in Connecticut, in the dual role of designer and supervisor of manufacturing and later for what would become MacGregor Golf. Some years after that, Willie also consulted with A.G. Spalding on their growing golf business.

Willie Dunn has been recognized for opening the country's first indoor golf teaching facility, which opened in 1895 at Madison Square Garden. There, he gave golf lessons in a large room that measured approximately 75 feet long by 30 feet wide, with a ceiling height of 28 feet and a strip of rubber matting that allowed up to six students to practice at one time.

As for Willie Campbell, he also grew up on the links of Musselburgh, learning about the game as a caddie and a player. In time, he became one of the most celebrated match-play golfers and developed a reputation as a highly competent course designer as well as a skilled ball- and club-maker, so perhaps it was not surprising when he received a combined offer in 1894 from the leaders of The Country Club in Brookline, Massachusetts, and the Essex Country Club on Boston's North Shore to travel to the United States to serve as their golf professional. The Country Club also requested that he revamp their course and expand it from six holes to nine.

The joint position worked well enough for a year, but then The Country Club asked Campbell to work there full-time. In addition to his duties as professional, he designed and completed a second nine.

Once that was done, Campbell moved to the nearby Myopia Hunt Club, and it was at that retreat he began turning to his wife, Georgina, for help. She, too, had been born and raised in Musselburgh and had developed into a fine player as well. At Myopia, she worked in the shop and assisted in the making of balls and clubs. She also became an active golf instructor, dealing mostly with youngsters and women. For those reasons, Georgina Campbell is considered to have been the first woman golf professional in America.

Recalling their beginnings in golf at Musselburgh, where access to courses was open, the Campbells formed a strong conviction that the American game needed to be similarly available if it was to prosper. That led them to approach city officials in Boston with a concept to construct a municipal golf course in Franklin Park, which had been laid out in the 1880s by the famous landscape architect Fredrick Law Olmstead. The idea was well received, and the city commissioned Willie Campbell to design a 9-hole track there and then to serve as its professional. That made him the first municipal course professional in the United States. It also allowed him to realize the Campbells' dream of bringing affordable golf to the everyday citizens. Over the next four years the Campbells worked side by side developing the game for all classes of Boston's citizens, and by 1900 golfers were playing 40,000 9-hole rounds a year there.

In a sad turn of fate, just as Willie Campbell found his niche in American golf, his health began to deteriorate. He passed away in the fall of 1900, at the age of 38. A number of people applied for Campbell's former job, but in reality, there was only one logical successor, his widow, Georgina. In the spring of 1901, she assumed the role as successor to her beloved Willie and over the next nine years successfully served in that position, at which point she transitioned to the role of club matron. It was a job she held until her retirement in 1926.

Over her 30 years at Franklin Park, Georgina Campbell welcomed thousands of golfers. Among those were two players who would go on to change the face of the American game and bolster its growth and popularity. One was a local caddie from a working-class family and the other a southerner from a more privileged upbringing who was attending Harvard. The local lad was Francis Ouimet, who would stun the golf world in 1913 by winning the U.S. Open at The Country Club, and the collegiate student was Bobby Jones, who made Franklin Park his "home course" when he was earning his B.A. in English literature at Harvard.

Another of the notable immigrant professionals was Willie Park Jr. The son of the first British Open Champion, Willie Jr. also grew up in Musselburgh. He, too, worked as a caddie at the links there and learned how to play the game on that track. By the time he turned 16, he had developed well enough as a player to enter his first Open Championship. The year was 1880, and he finished 16th, a single stroke behind his father.

A few years after that tournament, Park began to take an active role in his father's ball- and club-making business, Wm. Park & Son. He also continued competing, winning his first Open in 1887, at Prestwick. Two years later, Park captured his second Open Championship, this time on his home course at Musselburgh.

As the Wm. Park & Son business grew, Park's competitive game paid the price, as he took extended sabbaticals away from the golf course to concentrate on developing the family business. Through the 1880s and into the 1890s, the operation grew from a professional's workshop into a small factory employing more than 80 workers. Day-to-day manufacturing came under the watchful eye of Willie's older brother Frank, while Park focused on developing new products. During that time, he received patents for a number of innovative irons, woods, and balls. Park also sought to drive the overall sales and revenues for the growing business in 1894 by establishing three additional retail branches, in Edinburgh, Scotland; London; and Manchester, England.

Around the same time, Willie Park Jr. came to realize that the introduction of golf in America presented other growth opportunities for his family's business as well as his fledgling golf course design services. So, he ventured to the United States at the end of the 19th century to play in a series of exhibition matches against his old friends Willie Dunn Jr. and Willie Campbell, among others. Those matches gave Park outstanding exposure in American newspapers and magazines, leading him to establish an American branch of the Wm. Park & Son

OPPOSITE Francis Ouimet, *left*, and Jerry Travers are among only five golfers to win a U.S. Open as an amateur.

golf stores in New York City. They also helped him secure several commissions to design golf courses.

Park's design business in the United States truly bloomed with the onset of World War I and the sudden halt of new course construction in the British Isles. In 1916, offices for *Willie Park: Golf Architect* opened in North America, with a base in Montreal and satellite offices in New York and Toronto. He focused not only on detailed design, but construction services and management as well, forming alliances with major suppliers and contractors. Through the years, he was able to produce some memorable work, such as the North Course at Olympia Fields and the great track at the Maidstone Club in East Hampton, Long Island.

Park broke even more ground when he authored *The Game of Golf*, which is regarded as the first instructional book in the sport. Years after that, the man generally considered the finest flatstick player of his time released *The Art of Putting*, his teenage daughter Doris illustrating the tome with her drawings.

Sometimes, entire families made the trek to America. Such was the case with the Foulis brothers, David, James Jr., and Robert, who hailed from the ancient ecclesiastic center of St. Andrews. Their grandfather was a sheepherder who tended a flock used to maintain the grass on the course at the turn of the 19th century, and their father was an outstanding club-maker who worked as a foreman in Old Tom Morris's golf shop. Not surprisingly, the lads developed a strong love for golf, thanks largely to their proximity to the Old Course and their easy access to equipment. It also didn't hurt having Old Tom school them on the game.

It was Charles Blair Macdonald, often referred to as the Father of American Golf, who was responsible for bringing the Foulis family to the States. After opening his Chicago Golf Club in 1892, Macdonald reached out to Old Tom Morris for a recommendation for a golf professional at his nascent retreat. Macdonald had gotten to know Old Tom well while he was studying at St. Andrews University in the early 1870s and valued his opinion. Old Tom immediately thought of the Foulis brothers. Macdonald first offered the job to the eldest of the boys, Robert, but he was otherwise engaged as a caddie master at a club near Glasgow, so Macdonald reached out to James, who happily accepted. James was 24 years old, and when he arrived at Chicago Golf, he became the first professional in the Midwest.

In addition to his work as the professional at Chicago Golf, Foulis began designing courses. His first project was a 9-hole layout on Chicago's North Shore. First known as Lake Forest Golf Club, it later became the Onwentsia Club. At the beginning of the process, Foulis asked his brother Robert to lend a hand on the

k Hutchison
ng the Brit-
pen cham-
hip at St.
ews by sink-
final putt on
ighteenth
n (arrow
to Hutchi-

wood & Under-
wood.

Jock Hutchison of Chicago holding the British op
championship trophy, which he brought with him to
United States, emblematic of America's golfing triumph
International

construction project. This time, Robert could get away, and once the layout was completed, in 1896, he accepted the professional/greenkeeper position there. Two years later, he and brother James collaborated on a second nine.

The two brothers returned to Scotland in December of 1895 for three months. When they trekked back to the States in the spring of 1896, they brought their brother David, and he went to work as a full-time club-maker for James at Chicago Golf Club, while Robert returned to Lake Forest.

With Robert and James prospering in the United States, the rest of the Foulis family decided to relocate to the Chicago area, with the

patriarch James Sr. They arrived in 1898, with James Sr. joining James Jr. and David at Chicago Golf Club and setting up what came to be an innovative and prestigious ball- and club-making and supply business.

The Foulis Golf Shop became a center of creativity, exemplified by the work that James and David did to modify and greatly improve the performance of the revolutionary Haskell golf ball, by adding exterior dimples to what had been a fairly smooth exterior as a way of enhancing carry and bounce. The brothers also crafted a totally new style of iron that filled a gap between the traditional mashie that was similar to today's 5-iron and the niblick, which was close

The New York Times covered the action from St. Andrews, where Scottish-born U.S. citizen Jack "Jock" Hutchison Sr., *above and right*, won the 1921 Open Championship in a 36-hole playoff. Hutchison also won the 1920 PGA Championship and the 1937 and 1947 PGA Seniors Championships.

to the loft of a modern 9-iron. The name for their new club, for which they received a patent, seemed only logical: mashie-niblick. For the next 16 years, the brothers enjoyed income from every one manufactured and sold.

David is also credited with introducing the cup liner to the States. A combination of cup and flagstick known as the Foulis Flag, it was the first product to hold a flagstick in a perfectly upright position.

Not surprisingly, the brothers proved themselves to be strong players. James Jr. won the second U.S. Open ever played, at Shinnecock Hills on Long Island in 1896, and competed in 11 of the first 12 national championships. Brother Robert entered four U.S. Opens, and David one.

Golf was in its infancy in America when the Foulis brothers ventured to the New World, and they contributed a great deal to the early growth and success of the game there. In addition to being top players, the boys created nearly 50 new golf course designs in the States, served what were some of the first and most important clubs in the land, gave instruction to hundreds of budding players, and secured patents for some of the most significant technological innovations in golf club and ball development in the history of the game. They also took leadership roles in regional golf associations and studied agronomy so the golf clubs and courses they served could offer the best possible conditions.

The Smiths were another clan that came to the States at the turn of the 20th century. The first to arrive was Alex, and his brothers Willie, George, and Macdonald soon followed. They were the sons of the longtime greenkeeper on the Carnoustie links, and the three eldest served as apprentices there to the legendary professional Bob Simpson.

Alex headed to the United States in the spring of 1898, to work at the Washington Park Club in Chicago. It did not take him long to impress his new employers as a teacher and club-maker, and also as a player when he finished second in the U.S. Open at the Myopia Hunt Club that year.

Smith spent his first winters in California, toiling for the Coronado Golf Club in San Diego and then at the Los Angeles Country Club. In 1901, he took the professional's position at the Nassau Country Club on Long Island, and it was there that he taught and mentored an immensely talented young golfer named Jerry Travers, who would go on to win four U.S. Amateurs and the 1915 U.S. Open.

Early in America's golf history, clubs developed a strong affinity for players who competed at the highest levels. Strong member pride and new member recruiting were often developed around their professional's playing record, and they sought out the best. Alex Smith became an especially hot property after he won the 1906 U.S. Open as well as the inaugural Metropolitan Open the year before and a couple of prestigious Western Open Championships. In 1906, he took a winter job as the first professional at the Atlanta Athletic Club at East Lake. Then, after eight years at Nassau, Smith accepted an offer to be the golf professional of the Wykagyl Country Club in New Rochelle, New York, in 1908. Two years later, he captured another U.S. Open title and by 1913 had added three more Met Open trophies to his collection.

For a time, Smith also worked at the Shennecossett Golf Club in Groton, Connecticut, commuting between that retreat and Wykagyl, about 100 miles to the west. During his tenure there, he once again demonstrated that he was as skilled an instructor and nurturer of golf talent as he was a player. That was the result of his taking a promising young female golfer named Glenna Collett and helping her develop into one of the greatest amateur players in the history of golf. She won six U.S. Women's Amateur titles in her career and played on four Curtis Cup teams while captaining two. In time, she earned the much-deserved moniker of "The Bobby Jones of women's golf."

The second of the Smith brothers, Willie, followed Alex only a few weeks after he had immigrated from Carnoustie to Chicago, as a result of an offer to be the professional at Shinnecock Hills on the northern tip of New York's Long Island. That same year, they both competed in the U.S. Open at Myopia, with Alex finishing second and Willie just 5 strokes behind. The next year, Willie moved to the Chicago area to take over as the professional at the newly opened Midlothian Country Club, quickly distinguishing himself as a player by capturing the first-ever Western Open and then winning the 1899 U.S. Open at the Baltimore Country Club by a margin of 11 strokes, setting a record that would not be broken until the year 2000, when Tiger Woods won at Pebble Beach by 15 shots.

Macdonald, the youngest of the Smith brothers, was 20 years old when he emigrated from Scotland, in March of 1908. He, too, was a strong player and went to work as an assistant professional to his brother George at the Claremont Country Club in north Oakland, California.

Just two years later, Mac, as he was often called, played in his first U.S. Open, at the Philadelphia Cricket Club, joined in the field by brothers George and Alex. It was the first of many majors for Mac, and at the end of regulation play, he and Alex were tied for the lead with American prodigy John McDermott. The three engaged in an 18-hole playoff, with Alex prevailing. McDermott came in second, with Mac finishing third.

Mac Smith continued to operate out of Claremont, where one of his primary duties was giving lessons. One of his pupils was a youngster named Jack Neville, whose father was the club

greenkeeper. In 1912, Neville won the inaugural California State Amateur; it was the first of his five wins in that championship. Neville also went on to play on the 1923 Walker Cup squad, but he is probably best known for laying out the fabled Pebble Beach Golf Links with fellow amateur standout Douglas Grant.

Mac made his second venture on the national competitive stage when he traveled to Chicago for the 1912 Western Open, which in those days was regarded as a major. Mac came out on top, besting a field that included his brother Alex. The next year, Mac moved east to join Alex at the Wykagyl Golf Club. Then he took the professional's job at the Oakmont Country Club outside Pittsburgh. Playing out of that fine retreat, Mac garnered another prestigious golf title by winning the Met Open.

Mac seemed to disappear from view for most of World War I but resurfaced in a big way after marrying Louise Harvey, who was described in a newspaper account of the nuptials as being "a charming woman of both ability and fortune." It seems that fortune made it easier for Smith to concentrate on his playing. He teed it up in the 1924 Open Championship at Hoylake, coming in third, and the U.S. Open that year, finishing tied for fourth. Mac Smith still had it, and remarkably he hung on to it for several years to come, as evidenced by his putting in runner-up performances at both those tourneys in 1930, the year Bobby Jones achieved his remarkable Grand Slam.

George Smith is the least known of the Smith brothers. He followed Alex and Willie to the United States a year after they had, in 1899, and he took his first golf job at the San Rafael Country Club in California. For many years after that, he served as the club professional at the Claremont Country Club in Oakland and found time to enter three U.S. Opens, each of which had his siblings in the fields. George also worked

OPPOSITE Bobby Jones's golf swing was a study in fluidity, one of many skills that enabled him to complete an improbable sweep of golf's Grand Slam events in 1930. **ABOVE** Dressed and driven for success: Jock Hutchison, *left*, and Jock Hutchison Jr. at the Glen View Club in Golf, Illinois.

for a spell as Willie's assistant at Midlothian, and he hired Mac at Claremont. Later, they joined forces as professionals at the new Del Monte Golf and Country Club. George also helped out his older brother Alex at Belleair Country Club in Florida during the winter season of 1917.

Members of the Anderson family from the East Lothian region of Scotland also ventured to the States at the end of the 19th century, the first of which was Willie Law Anderson, who was only 16 years old when he emigrated to the United States, arriving at Ellis Island in New York in March of 1896. His father, Thomas, was the head greenkeeper at North Berwick in Scotland, and young Willie was already well acquainted with the game. He had started caddying on the links

at North Berwick when he was 11 years old, and by the time he was 14 he was an apprentice club-maker in the nearby town of Gullane.

Anderson assumed his first professional position within a few days of landing in New York, at the Misquamicut Club at Watch Hill, Rhode Island. Soon, members there entrusted him with the task of extending the club's original 9-hole course, which had been designed by the noted Musselburgh professional Willie Park Jr., to 18.

Misquamicut was only the first of what would turn out to be many clubs that Anderson served in America, as he also found work in later years at the Baltusrol Golf Club in New Jersey, the Country Club of Pittsfield in western

Massachusetts, the Onwentsia Club in Chicago, the St. Louis Country Club in Missouri, and the Philadelphia Cricket Club. Later in his career, Anderson spent winters in Florida, working for Henry Flagler and the East Coast Railway, at the Ponce de León Hotel in the historic town of St. Augustine. Anderson was lauded for his teaching skills as well as for his club-making. However, it was his talent as a competitive player that truly set him apart.

A year after he arrived in the United States, Anderson entered his first U.S. Open, in 1897, at the Chicago Golf Club. Remarkably, the teenager finished second, a stroke back. Four years later, Anderson won the event in a playoff at the Myopia Hunt Club outside Boston. Then, the man who was described as dour and businesslike on the golf course went on a run the likes of which has never been seen in golf, winning three consecutive U.S. Opens, in 1903, 1904, and 1905. No one has since been able to duplicate that feat. It wasn't just his play in the national championship that distinguished Anderson as a player. He also won four Western Opens, which at the time was regarded as the second most important tournament in American professional golf.

Within four years of Willie's arrival, his father, Tom, made the trip, leaving behind his wife and four young daughters but bringing his then 14-year-old son Tom Jr. Tom Sr. quickly secured a professional's job at the Montclair Golf Club in New Jersey and held that position until his death in 1913. He was best known for his innovations as a teacher, which included being the first golf professional ever to use a mirror as a teaching aid. He also played in two U.S. Opens.

As for Tom Jr., he went to work for his father at Montclair for a couple of years and later succeeded his brother Willie as the professional at Pittsfield. After that, Tom Jr. held jobs at the Inwood Country Club outside New York City and the Oakmont Country Club in the Pittsburgh area. He returned to Montclair when his father died and was working there when he was killed in a car accident, in 1915. He was only 30 years old.

Young Tom was never the player his brother was, but he was good enough to play in nine U.S. Opens and finish in the top 10 three times. He was known as a big hitter, as well as a fashion plate; the flashy and dashing clothes he wore on the golf course inspired a young professional named Walter Hagen to dress that same stylish way later in his career.

Then, there were three Maiden brothers, all raised in Carnoustie and all drawn to the game of golf. They received their first introduction to the sport by caddying on the links in that seaside town, and they learned about playing, teaching, and club-making from the great Carnoustie professional Robert Simpson. The two eldest boys, James and Stewart, who were also known as Jimmy and Kiltie respectively, emigrated to the States and became best known for their relationships and interactions with the great American amateur Bobby Jones. The youngest, Allan, moved to Australia, where he became a leading instructor. Among his students was five-time British Open Champion Peter Thomson.

It was the celebrated Scottish golf professional Alex Smith, on a visit to his hometown of Carnoustie, who induced Jimmy Maiden to head across the Atlantic to the States. Smith had just accepted his first head professional position, at the prestigious Nassau Country Club near New York City, and was looking for someone to assist him. He believed that his 20-year-old brother-in-law Jimmy Maiden was the perfect candidate and quickly convinced him to take the job.

OPPOSITE Twenty-year-old American amateur Francis Ouimet, *center*, with British professionals Harry Vardon, *left*, and Ted Ray, *right*, prior to their 18-hole playoff at the 1913 U.S. Open Championship, which Ouimet won by 5 strokes.

The two worked together for three years at Nassau before Maiden took his first head position, at the Youngstown Country Club in Ohio. Then, he went to work as the professional for the Inverness Club in Toledo. In addition, Maiden traveled to Atlanta for a couple of winters to serve alongside Smith at the newly opened East Lake Golf Club outside Atlanta. When Smith decided that he needed to concentrate on his job at Nassau and make that a full-time job, he recommended that the folks at East Lake hire Maiden as his replacement.

Maiden stayed at East Lake only through the beginning of 1908, at which point he agreed to fill a sudden opening for a head professional at Nassau after his mentor and brother-in-law decided to move on, but he had been in Atlanta long enough to give lessons to a local lawyer named Robert P. Jones and fashion a cut-down club for his young son, Bobby, who was showing an interest in the game.

As Maiden returned to Long Island, he considered who might replace him at East Lake. He immediately thought of his younger brother, Stewart. The club took Maiden's recommendation, and Stewart left Scotland for Atlanta in the winter of 1908.

Jimmy Maiden quickly settled into his new job at Nassau and became a highly regarded instructor. While he enjoyed his new life in New York, he also stayed in touch with some of the people he had met in Atlant,a like Bobby Jones, the young boy for whom he fashioned that cut-down club.

In the years since Maiden had worked at East Lake, Jones had become one of the best amateur players in the world. In the summer of 1923, Jones paid Jimmy Maiden a visit as he prepared for the U.S. Open that was being played that year at the nearby Inwood Country Club.

Jones was complaining about his putting, and after working with him for a bit, Maiden suggested he try a putter he had in his shop. The club had been forged in Scotland around the turn of the century and bore the cleek-maker's mark of a rose, signifying that St. Andrews master iron-maker Robert Condie had made it. After hitting putts from all over the green with it, Jones said, "Jim, I really like this club." Maiden put three balls down on the green, ranging in distance from the hole from 8 to 10 feet. "Bob, put these three putts in the hole, and the putter is yours," he said. As the third and final ball dropped, Jones assumed possession of what was to become one of the most famous clubs in golf history. Jimmy Maiden had a common practice of naming his favorite clubs. His driver was known as "Long Tom," and the putter he had just gifted Jones bore the appellation "Calamity Jane."

Jones used Calamity Jane to win at Inwood and then to triumph in the 1924 and 1925 U.S. Amateurs. As the original club head started to wear, Jones decided to have replicas made. He asked J. Victor East, a golf professional and club-maker at Spalding, to produce six near-identical remakes of Calamity Jane. It is believed that after testing each of them, Jones decided on just one of the copies, giving the balance to friends. He then put Calamity Jane II into play, collecting 10 more major wins with that flatstick, from 1926 through his Grand Slam season of 1930.

Born five years after big brother Jimmy, in 1886, Kiltie was 22 years old when he traveled to the States, and the East Lake Country Club, to replace his brother at that Atlanta retreat. The younger Maiden was a strong player and a solid instructor, and he quickly began working with a pair of East Lake's junior players. One was Alexa Stirling, who was 10 years old at the time of his arrival and would go on to win three consecutive U.S. Women's Amateurs. The other was a 6-year-old prodigy named Bobby Jones.

A year before Kiltie's arrival, Jones got his start in the game by swinging with a single, yet expertly cut-off club fashioned by Maiden's brother, Jimmy. Once the younger Maiden started work at East Lake, Jones began building his game by mimicking Kiltie's swing. Some claim Jones never took a formal lesson, and that may very well be true. There is no doubt, however, that Kiltie was a huge influence in the development of Jones's game. The impressionable youngster copied Maiden's technique to near perfection and considered the Scotsman his mentor. Maiden also gave his youthful protégé the confidence that he would always be there if and when he was needed. Either in person, or via telegram or phone call, Maiden assisted Jones whenever his game faltered.

Jones and Maiden continued their close golfing relationship until the amateur great retired from competitive play, with the professional frequently traveling with Jones to the major championships he entered. The noted golf writer O.B. Keeler dubbed Maiden "Kiltie the Kingmaker," and he is credited with being the first teacher to regularly accompany a student to tournaments.

St. Andrean Jock Hutchison was another immigrant professional, but he took a much more circuitous route to the United States, coming to America via Australia. A talented player who had grown up caddying and playing on the Old Course, he traveled Down Under in 1903 to work as a golf equipment salesman. He also gave lessons and exhibitions and even designed the course at the Australia Golf Club, which is celebrated today as the oldest in that land.

Then, in 1905, Hutchison accepted an offer to work as a golf professional for the W. C. Carnegie family at their compound on Cumberland Island off the coast of Georgia. It was something of a strange development, for Hutchison's older brother Tom had designed and built the private, 9-hole course there five years before. He had

also been employed as the Carnegie's coach and instructor, but in December of 1900, Tom was killed in a horseback-riding accident.

What that meant was when Jock made his way to Cumberland Island, he was essentially filling his late brother's old job. Eventually, he also took the job of professional at the Saint Andrews Golf Club in New York, where Andrew Carnegie was a prominent member.

As was the case with many golf professionals of that era, Hutchison was so much in demand that he moved around quite a bit, working at the Pittsburgh Golf Club for a spell and then jumping to the nearby Allegheny Country Club. In 1916, he settled in the Chicago area as the head professional at the Glen View Club, staying there until his retirement in 1953.

Hutchison was much prized for his teaching abilities, but what really appealed to many clubs in the early days was having a professional who could play. He competed in his first U.S. Open in 1905, and he finished in the top 10 in four of the first eight national championships he entered.

In 1916, Hutchison finished second in the U.S. Open and later that year played in the first PGA Championship, at the Siwanoy Country Club, just outside New York City. The tournament's format then was match play, and Hutchison made it to the finals, where he met Long Jim Barnes. Hutchison got off to a fast start in the 36-hole match, running to a 4-up lead after the first eight holes, but he ended up falling 1-down, on the 36th hole.

Hutchison had to wait for the beginning of a new decade for his first major title, and it came in the 1920 PGA Championship, which he won at the Flossmoor Country Club in suburban Chicago. That month, the Glen View Club professional also captured the Western Open and finished runner-up in the U.S. Open, leading many observers to regard him as the finest player in the United States, but the Scotsman secured

ABOVE Walter Hagen won the 1921 PGA Championship at Inwood Country Club in Far Rockaway, New York, the first of his first PGA titles. **OPPOSITE** Glenna Collett Vare won six U.S. Women's Amateur Championships among her 49 victories. The Vare Trophy, named in her honor, recognizes the LPGA professional with the lowest scoring average.

what might have been an even bigger triumph that year when he became a U.S. citizen.

It had to have been a career highlight for Jock to return home to St. Andrews to play in his first British Open Championship, in 1921, nearly 20 years after he had emigrated from Scotland. He was going to be competing in his hometown on the hallowed Old Course before friends and family and for what at the time was the most coveted championship in the game, and he could hardly hide his excitement.

Hutchison had the advantage of knowing the Old Course intimately. He was also able to secure one of St. Andrews' best caddies, John Melville, who had been a favorite of Old Tom Morris, to carry his bag. The only real question was whether Hutchison, at the age of 37, could stave off the youngsters.

For the first two rounds, Jock played with a young American amateur named Robert Tyre "Bobby" Jones. Jock played well enough to hold a 1-shot lead after 36 holes. After finishing tied with amateur Roger Wethered after 72 holes, Hutchison prevailed in a 36-hole playoff. And while some in the British press may have disagreed, the U.S. media proclaimed him to be the first American winner of the Open Championship—and now the greatest golfer in the world. In addition to being regarded as an individual triumph for Jock Hutchison, his win in the 1921 Open Championship is looked upon as representing the time when dominance in the game moved from Great Britain to America, and Yanks proceeded to win 12 of the next 13 British Opens.

One of the things that made Scotsman Charles "Chay" Burgess unique was that he came into golf quite late in life. To be sure, he had caddied and learned to play the game as a young boy in the village of Montrose, but it wasn't until he was 28 years old that he decided to give up his life as a professional footballer and become a golf professional instead, taking a job at the Royal Albert Golf Club in his hometown.

Several years later, Burgess traveled what was becoming a well-worn path for Scottish professionals by immigrating to America, to accept a position at the Woodland Golf Club in Newton, Massachusetts, outside Boston. Shortly after his arrival at Woodland, Burgess was surprised to find a group of young golfers one day playing the course. Burgess was instantly taken by one of the lads, and they soon formed a teacher-student relationship, often playing together on Sunday afternoons. Burgess even furnished the teenager with equipment from his shop. The young man was named Francis Ouimet. Born to immigrant parents, he regularly looped at The Country Club in nearby Brookline and played countless rounds of golf there.

Burgess and Ouimet worked together for several years, and in the spring of 1913, the young golfer won the Massachusetts Amateur, just weeks after his 20th birthday. Later that year, Ouimet made it to match play in the U.S. Amateur, losing his second match to the eventual winner, Jerome Travers. On the basis of that performance, the United States Golf Association asked Ouimet to play in the U.S. Open, which was being held at The Country Club two weeks later.

Ouimet happily accepted the invitation and then produced perhaps the greatest upset in the history of golf, finishing in a tie with the great English professionals Harry Vardon and Ted Ray at the end of regulation play and then beating them in a playoff.

Ouimet's success in competitive golf did not end with that U.S. Open triumph. He would go on to collect a total of six Massachusetts Amateur titles and two U.S. Amateurs, the second of which would come in 1931, at the age of 38. Ouimet also played on eight Walker Cup teams and captained four. In 1951, the young man who Chay Burgess had watched practice on his Woodland golf course was named Captain of the Royal and Ancient Golf Club of St. Andrews, the first American to be given this special recognition.

The influence of early immigrant professionals delivered the necessary knowledge to nurture the American game from infancy to a thriving sport. They educated and subsequently inspired a whole new generation of players, like Bobby Jones and Francis Ouimet. Their mentees would turn out to be the first generation of homebred golf professionals, who would be charged to take golf in America to the next level.

The most likely candidate for the honor of America's first homebred professional is John Shippen Jr. Born December 5, 1879, in Washington, D.C., Shippen was an African-American and one of nine children. His father was an elementary school teacher, who returned to school to obtain a theology degree from Howard University in Washington, DC. Following graduation he accepted his first ministerial position, in Arkansas. Work compelled him to relocate to Mississippi after that, and then, in 1893, the elder Shippen moved his family to the Shinnecock Indian Reservation on the northern tip of Long Island, near Southampton, New York.

It was there that 13-year-old John had his first brush with the game, working on a course construction crew at the Shinnecock Hills Golf Club and serving as a caddie, which would become as favored an entry into golf in the United States as it had been in Scotland. He is also said to have learned how to play the game at that time from Shinnecock's Scottish golf professional Willie Dunn Jr. Shippen became so proficient at golf

that Dunn made him his assistant, also teaching him along the way to make clubs and give lessons.

The U.S. Open was contested for only the second time in 1896, and the venue was Shinnecock Hills, which Dunn had updated and expanded to 18 holes the year before. Among those in the field of 35 was Shippen. Only 16 years old, he finished tied for fifth, earning a $25 share of the $335 purse.

That performance bolstered Shippen's reputation as a player and demonstrated that he was good enough to compete with the best of the immigrant professionals. He was able to find good work in the game even though he was African-American and had to contend with Jim Crow laws that further enabled racial discrimination in the United States. It is believed that his first position on his own was in the late 1890s as a private instructor to the prosperous Frederick Cromwell family of New York City, who had a summer residence in Bernardsville, New Jersey. Then, in 1899 and with the strong endorsement of Dunn, Philadelphia's Aronimink Golf Club hired Shippen as their professional. Records show that by September 1900, Shippen was playing out of New York City's Marine and Field Club located in Brooklyn and known today as the Dyker Beach Golf Course.

Shippen returned to Long Island and the Maidstone Club in 1902 and stayed there for 11 years. His next role was as a private swing coach to industrialist Henry C. Frick and future New Jersey U.S. Senator J. S. Frelinghuysen. During this engagement, it is believed that Shippen worked out of Spring Lake Golf Club in New Jersey. Then, in 1916, Shippen went back home, in a sense, to Shinnecock, only this time he served solely as the golf course superintendent. It was during this time that C. B. Macdonald and his assistant, civil engineer Seth Raynor, were hired

In 1937, Augusta National Golf Club hosted the inaugural PGA Seniors Championship (now the Senior PGA Championship presented by KitchenAid). Gathered around the Alfred S. Bourne Trophy, *left to right*, were club members Paul Paulson and Alex Cunningham, Prosper J. Berckmans, whose family's nursery property became Augusta National, contestants William Sherwood and John Inglis flanking the trophy, Captain Thomas Clark, eventual tournament champion Jock Hutchison, and Fielding Wallace, a charter member of Augusta National and later a USGA President.

to do a redesign of the golf course there, and they seemed to have been so impressed with Shippen's work that they induced him to take that very same position at the neighboring National Golf Links of America, which Macdonald and Raynor had built a few years earlier on adjoining property.

After a couple of years at the National, Shippen left golf for a government work, assuming an office position in Washington, DC, with the Department of Public Lands. After four or five years in the nation's capital, the call of the game and the desire to work out of doors drew him to golf once again, and he assisted in building "a course for Negroes near Laurel, Maryland" at the National Capitol Country Club. Once it opened, Shippen worked in the clubhouse and gave lessons.

His next position, as the professional at Shady Rest Golf and Country Club in Scotch Plains, New Jersey, would be his longest and his last. A group of African-American investors had purchased the retreat, and it became the country's first complete, full-service country club for persons of color, drawing most of its members from northern and central New Jersey as well as Manhattan and Brooklyn. In 1931 club leaders hired Shippen as their professional, a position he held for the next 28 years. He retired in 1959 when he was 80 years old.

In gauging how golf was progressing in the United States, observers of the game often looked at the performances of the homebred professionals in major championships. That told them how well the Americans were getting to know the sport, and how quickly they were picking it up. The sense was a New World professional would never be considered on the same level as the immigrant professional until he won the U.S. Open.

The man who finally broke through was John Joseph McDermott. Best known as "Johnny" or "JJ," he won the 1911 U.S. Open, at Chicago Golf

Club, and then captured his second national championship the following year.

The son of an Irish mail carrier, McDermott was born in West Philadelphia on August 12, 1891. He was only nine years old when he started caddying at the Aronimink Golf Club, which was located just across the street from his grandfather's farm. Small in physical stature, McDermott never grew taller than 5 feet 8 inches or weighed more than 135 pounds. Even though he was a good student, McDermott dropped out of high school after his sophomore year at the encouragement of his father, who deemed it was time for Johnny to find a fit trade for life. Much to his father's dismay, McDermott felt his future was his golf, and he quickly accepted an offer to be an assistant professional in 1906 at Camden Country Club in New Jersey. The following year, he moved to a head position as the professional at Merchantville Field Club in Cherry Hill, New Jersey, which he held over the next three seasons through 1910.

In 1909, McDermott entered his first U.S. Open. Only 18 years old, he finished in a tie for 49th. It was not exactly a sterling debut, but it did nothing to sap his confidence. The bold and brash young McDermott was not at all shy about taking on more established players in challenge matches when he was not teeing it up in tournaments.

McDermott played considerably better in the 1910 U.S. Open, which was played at the Philadelphia Cricket Club. By the end of the regulation 72-hole competition, he was in a tie for first place, with the great Scotsman Alex Smith and his younger brother Mac. It was the first three-way playoff in U.S. Open history, and the elder Smith prevailed, beating McDermott by 4 shots and his brother by 6.

McDermott was representing the Atlantic City Country Club as its professional when he teed it in the 1911 U.S. Open, at the Chicago Golf Club. Once again, he found himself in a three-way tie for first place at the end of 72 holes. This time, though, he prevailed, triumphing over Mike Brady and George Simpson. It was a momentous win, for it made McDermott the first American ever to win the national championship and ended the British professionals' 16-year domination of the U.S. Open. Even more impressive, he accomplished the feat at the age of 19 years, 10 months, and 12 days to become the youngest winner, a record that stands to this day.

The following year, at the Country Club of Buffalo in New York, McDermott became only the second player to become a two-time winner of the U.S. Open, and the first golfer ever to post a subpar total in that tournament. McDermott was only 20 years old when he sealed that victory. He seemed to be on top of the golfing world, especially after he played in his first British Open Championship the next year, in the summer of 1913, placing fifth, the highest finish an American had ever managed in that esteemed event. Soon, however, his life started to fall apart.

Only weeks before he was to defend his U.S. Open title at The Country Club at Brookline, McDermott secured an 8-shot win at the Shawnee Open. He directed his victory speech at visiting British professionals Harry Vardon and Ted Ray, and USGA leaders took those comments as an inappropriate challenge. In fact, they were so miffed by McDermott's behavior that the USGA considered rejecting his tournament application for the national championship, but they relented only days before the event. What nobody other than McDermott knew at the time was that he was battling another, even more serious problem, having lost his life savings earlier that year as a result of ill-advised investments.

On November 1, 1913, a short notice appeared in *The New York Times*: "John J. McDermott, open golf champion of 1911-1912 and present holder of the Western title, is suffering from a nervous breakdown. He became very ill last night and his parents had him removed to a private hospital in Philadelphia." McDermott made several attempts over the next two years to rebound from his breakdown to return to competitive golf but was never able to successfully do so. In June of 1916, his family formally committed him to a state hospital for the insane at Norristown, Pennsylvania. America's first great homebred professional champion was only 24 years old, and his golf career appeared to have come to an untimely end. The eventual diagnosis was noted as "chronic schizophrenia," a medical condition first named only a few years earlier, in 1911.

Word of McDermott's commitment spread through the game, and many of his fellow golf professionals came to visit him. Gene Sarazen made multiple trips to the state institution. Once, while he was in the area for an exhibition, Walter Hagen visited the facility to check on McDermott, who was an early inspiration. The hospital was built on 265 acres of rolling hills, and McDermott created a simple course with six holes there and regularly played over the 1,232-yard layout. Hagen accompanied him on one of those rounds.

In 1971, 60 years after his historic U.S. Open victory in Chicago, McDermott quietly traveled the Merion Golf Club for that year's national championship. He was thin and shabbily dressed. Failing to recognize he was the great former champion, an assistant professional assumed by his appearance that he didn't belong in the golf shop and proceeded to escort him out. Arnold Palmer recognized McDermott and quickly assured the young assistant that everything was all right. Then Palmer took McDermott aside; according to golf historian John Coyne, "They talked golfer to golfer, champion to champion, and Palmer arranged for McDermott to stay at the tournament as his special guest."

That was McDermott's last visit to a major championship. Only weeks later, he passed in his sleep at the Norristown facility, just 11 days short of his 80th birthday.

The Early Years
of the PGA of America

Born to blue-collar Irish immigrants in Brookline, Massachusetts, Tom McNamara quickly ascended through the caddie ranks at a couple of neighborhood courses when he was a young boy and secured his first job as golf professional when he was only 17. It was quite a rise, and for many years, he worked at clubs in and around the Boston area, developing into one of the most competitive of the first homebred professionals, finishing second in the U.S. Open in 1909 and 1912 and tying for fifth in 1910.

Eventually, McNamara moved to New York City, where he accepted a position as the golf equipment representative at the Wanamaker Store. It was during a sales meeting there that he brought up the idea of organizing American golf professionals into a formal association. Golf was becoming more and more popular in the States, as newer players took up the game and new places for them to play started coming on line, and McNamara thought his fellow professionals could benefit from working together. His boss, Rodman Wanamaker, saw merit in the idea, in part because he believed it would improve the lot of golf professionals, whom club members and leaders often treated as second-class citizens. Ever the businessman, Wanamaker also saw an association of golf professionals as something that would advance and promote a constituency

that could help sell his golf gear. Wanamaker asked McNamara to put together a luncheon of prominent amateur and professional players to consider the idea.

Contrary to popular legend, the Taplow Club was not a dinner club, eatery, or meeting establishment. Rather it was Wanamaker's own nickname for an informal organization of "golf bugs" that originated in his Manhattan store. Wanamaker derived its title from Taplow Court, site of his home in London. The ninth-floor restaurant tables of the Wanamaker Store were decorated with real heather and Scottish plaid. It set the mood for a momentous luncheon on January 17, 1916.

Among those attending were amateur golfing great Francis Ouimet; noted writer, player, and budding course architect A. W. Tillinghast;

and P. C. Pulver, the *New York Evening Sun* reporter and one of the first newspapermen dedicated to covering the game of golf on a regular basis. Also seated at the table were some of America's top professionals, such as Walter Hagen, Alex Smith, James Maiden, Robert White, Jack Mackie, and Alex Pirie, and they represented both those who made their livings playing tournaments as well as the men who derived their livelihoods from their jobs at private and public golf facilities. The response to creating such a body was positive, and additional meetings followed. On April 10, in the second-floor boardroom of the Hotel Martinique on 32nd and Broadway, The Professional Golfers' Association of America formally came into existence. There were 78 members elected that day, including 35 charter members.

Several topics were raised at that initial luncheon. One was to give golf professionals a say when it came to the organization and staging of tournaments. Another included the establishment of a career placement mechanism to bring together unemployed professionals with clubs that had open positions. The members of the nascent group also discussed a program to aid professionals who suffered "at the hands of the club members who are lax in the payment of the professional for his services and supplies."

In addition to being the inspiration behind the meeting, and picking up the lunch tab, Wanamaker announced he would donate both a cup and prize money for a "worldwide tournament to be conducted along the plan of the News of the World tournament held abroad, where the players qualify in districts and the survivors meet at some appointed course to finish the tournament at match play." That competition came to be the PGA Championship, and the cup that golfers received for winning it was the Wanamaker Trophy.

Organizers then formed a seven-man group whose primary task was to define tentative bylaws for the new group. They named James Hepburn, a former secretary to the British PGA, to chair an organizational committee of professionals that included professionals Maiden, White, and Mackie as well Gilbert Nicholls, John Hobens, and Herbert Strong. Interestingly, none of them was American-born. This group also drafted a constitution, turning to the recently formed British PGA for assistance in that matter.

Initially, there were seven PGA Sections: Metropolitan, Middle States, New England, Southeastern, Central, Northwestern, and Pacific. The new PGA members referred to assistants who lacked the training for full membership as apprentices and designated additional classifications for salesmen and unemployed professionals.

The PGA's first Organizing Annual Meeting was held that summer at the Radisson Hotel in Minneapolis, coinciding with the playing of the 1916 U.S. Open Championship at the nearby Minikahda Club and running over two days. Members of the original seven Sections had formed executive committees by that time, and those committees elected Metropolitan Section Head Robert White as the PGA's first national president. He served in that position for three years.

Born in St. Andrews, White was the son of a blacksmith who went on to become a renowned cleek-maker, often producing iron heads for Old Tom Morris. White took up golf as a young

man and became friends with a young man from the northern Scottish town of Dornoch named Donald Ross, who was working in St. Andrews as an apprentice to Old Tom and who would go on to become a celebrated player and club professional as well as a World Golf Hall of Fame course architect. Ross and young Robert White played many rounds together on the Old Course. They also spent prodigious amounts of time around Old Tom, learning about the royal and ancient game from the sporting sage and absorbing his views on the design and upkeep of courses. It was, to say the least, an advanced education in the game of golf.

White was just 20 years old when he emigrated to America in 1894. Though he described himself as a schoolteacher, he immediately went to work in golf, accepting a position as the professional and greenkeeper at a new 9-hole course in the

Four months after a group of prominent amateur and professional golfers gathered in the ninth-floor restaurant, *opposite*, of the Wanamaker Store in New York City, *above*, the Professional Golfers' Association of America was formally established on April 10, 1916.

Myopia Hunt Club in Hamilton, Massachusetts, north of Boston. A year later, he relocated to Cincinnati, Ohio, where he designed the 9-hole course at the Cincinnati Country Club and then served as the professional and greenkeeper there. The new club's first president was William Howard Taft, who just 12 years later would take on a leadership role with considerably greater responsibilities, as the 27th president of the United States.

White soon made another move, this time to the Louisville Golf Club in Kentucky. Then, in 1902, he ventured north, to the Chicago area, to fill a club professional position at the Ravisloe Country Club located in Homewood, Illinois. In his off-hours, he sought to expand his knowledge of agronomy by taking continuing education sessions in agriculture at the University of Wisconsin.

Early in his tenure in the Chicago area, White played three key leadership roles in bringing together area professionals for their mutual benefit and proffering advice on how they could best do their jobs. Back then, professionals often met informally on Mondays at the A. G. Spalding store in downtown Chicago, and it was there that they started what is believed to have been the first professional golfers' association created in the United States. It was known simply as The Professional Golfers' Association, and White served as the regional group's first president.

As an outstanding club-maker, White also helped organize a group of area professionals who stayed in the area during the winter months into a consortium of club-makers. Then, in 1905, White was involved in the creation of a third organization, the Western Professional Golfers' Association. Its primary objectives were to encourage tournament play, promote an interest in golf, and deliver a means for exercising and enforcing discipline among golf professionals in an effort to protect their images. Once again, White found himself in a management position, this time as chairman of its Executive Committee.

Given that background, it was not surprising that the founders of the PGA of America asked White to be its first president. By the time White assumed that position in 1916, he had moved back East to work as a club professional first at the Shawnee Country Club in Pennsylvania and later the Montclair Golf Club in New Jersey and Wykagyl in New Rochelle, New York. It was at Wykagyl that he reconnected with his old friend Donald Ross, and they revamped several holes on that parklands course. In 1927, they fashioned 27 holes at the Ocean Forest Country Club in Myrtle Beach, South Carolina.

Ross and White collaborated again 20 years later on one more project: the formation of the American Society of Golf Course Architects. Once again, White was blazing a trail.

Jack Mackie was also present at the creation of the PGA. He, too, was a native Scot, and he had been working in the metropolitan New York area as a golf professional for a dozen years at several different clubs when he attended that initial lunch at Wanamaker's. One year later, he was ensconced in the head professional's position at Inwood Country Club on Long Island, near what today is JFK International Airport. Mackie found a welcome home there and ended up spending the next three decades at that waterside retreat.

At Inwood, Mackie served as the host professional for the 1921 PGA Championship, which Walter Hagen won, and the 1923 U.S. Open, at which a 21-year-old Georgian named Bobby Jones captured his first major. While holding that position, Mackie also became

OPPOSITE Scotsman Donald Ross was named golf professional at Pinehurst in North Carolina in 1900; it was there that he began his legendary course design career.

deeply involved with the PGA of America. He succeeded Robert White as president in 1919, holding that job for a year before taking on a variety of other leadership positions in the organization, including that of treasurer, from 1927 to 1939.

Perhaps his greatest contributions to the Association came through his handling of its finances, which Herb Graffis addressed in his seminal history of the Association, *The PGA*, describing Mackie as "a sturdy, canny Scot who showed traditional genius in stretching the meager funds of the PGA and increasing its revenue. He was also a cool hand in helping settle arguments with an apt quotation . . . In its first twenty years of existence it could be said that the PGA was run more by the authority of quotations from Robert Burns than by citing *Robert's Rules of Order*."

Mackie suffered a stroke in 1950, at the age of 71, and died three years later. At the time of his passing, he was lauded for his contributions

to the game of golf and to ensuring the early success—and survival—of the PGA. One of his obituaries read: "Jack had to the highest degree the merits of the Scot-American pioneer pro. He was a beloved, frank, cheery, and competent gentleman sportsman who served well amateurs, his club and his brother pros."

Mackie's successor as PGA president was an Englishman named George Jonathan Sargent. Born in 1882 in the village of Dorking in Surrey, he garnered his knowledge about the game of golf as a caddie. He fell hard for the sport, and by the time he was 12, Sargent was serving as an apprentice to a professional and club-maker outside London. After six years there, he ventured to the Ganton Golf Club in North Yorkshire, to take a job as an assistant to reigning British Open champion Harry Vardon.

Sargent's first independent professional position came as personal instructor to Sir Edgar Vincent, a member at the time of the British Parliament. Two years later, Sargent became the head professional at the Dewsbury District Golf Club in Yorkshire, and four years after that, he emigrated to the New World, stopping first at Royal Ottawa Golf Club in Canada and then heading to the Hyde Manor Golf Club near Sudbury, Vermont. The historic resort had begun as a way station on the stagecoach line between Montreal and Albany, New York, and had come to feature a large hotel, an amusement hall with bowling and billiards, and a 9-hole golf course.

Shortly after assuming that position, Sargent traveled south to Englewood Golf Club in Englewood, New Jersey, to compete in the 1909 U.S. Open. Playing with confidence and verve and shooting 71 for the final round, he managed to produce a 4-stroke victory over Tom McNamara.

ABOVE One of the PGA of America's most ardent supporters was journalist Herb Graffis, *center*, pictured with Horton Smith, *left*, and Walter Hagen. Graffis became the namesake for a national PGA award honoring charitable outreach and player development. OPPOSITE Six-time Open Champion Harry Vardon became golf's first international celebrity in 1900 when he toured the United States and Canada with five-time Open Champion J. H. Taylor. Vardon played in more than 80 matches and capped his trip with a U.S. Open victory.

Sargent's four-round total of 290 set a new scoring record by 5 shots. That Open turned out to be his only career major championship, although he would capture another tournament of note, the Canadian Open, in 1912. In his competitive career, Sargent competed in 17 U.S. Opens, finishing in the top 10 six times. In 1934, he played in the inaugural Masters and would go on to make a total of nine appearances in that event, the last in 1958.

It was as a club professional, however, where Sargent really made his mark. He held that job at the esteemed Chevy Chase Club outside Washington, DC , from 1909 to 1914 and then moved to the Interlachen Country Club in Edina, Minnesota. While there, Sargent became a member of the newly formed PGA of America, and in 1921 he served the first of what would be five yearlong terms as PGA president. In that role, Sargent was a strong proponent of instruction and analysis of the golf swing as a main focus for the golf professional and headed a project that provided PGA members with slow-motion movies of the swings of Harry Vardon, Bobby Jones, and Joyce Wethered, an act that is regarded as the birth of the PGA Education Program.

After three years at Interlachen, Sargent accepted an offer to become the professional at the Scioto Country Club in Columbus, Ohio. While there, Sargent played an important role in securing the 1926 U.S. Open for Scioto Country Club, which Bobby Jones won, and serving for a spell as the head golf coach for the team at Ohio State, which was located in the same city. Sargent and Jones developed such a close relationship after the 1926 Open that Jones asked Sargent to become the professional at his home club of East Lake. Sargent moved there in 1932.

Sargent died in 1962, two months before his 80th birthday. Of his ten children, two, Jack and Harold, became golf professionals. In 1958, the PGA elected Harold president of the Association, and he held that position for two years, making the Sargents the first and only father and son ever to have run that organization.

St. Andrean Alexander Pirie joined the great Scottish golf migration to the States in 1902, taking a series of jobs at New York area clubs after his arrival, beginning with Forrest Hill in Newark and including Siwanoy and Sunningdale in Westchester County. In 1918, he relocated to Long Island to serve as the professional at the North Shore Country Club.

Pirie quickly established himself in the golf professional community and attended that Wanamaker lunch in New York at which the PGA of America was born. Shortly afterward, he became one of the 35 charter members and in 1919 was elected secretary-treasurer of the Association. After two years in that position, Pirie left the New York region for Chicago to work as head professional for the recently founded Old Elm Club, which was the first all-male golf club in America. Then, in 1927, the PGA of America elected Pirie as its president. Among his many accomplishments in that office was gaining support for an increase in national dues, from $10 to $50 annually. As a result, the PGA was able to hire its first paid executive, with Albert Gates coming on board as the Association's business administrator and legal advisor.

Having worked at Old Elm as both the head professional and greenkeeper, PGA President Pirie also sought to get his outfit to work more closely with the National Association of Greenkeepers of America as well as the National Association of Club Managers, arguing that they could more easily help the game grow and prosper by collaborating. In addition, Pirie, who also happened to be the brother-in-law of the

PGA's first president, Robert White, helped advance slow-motion filming of golf swings for member education purposes, predicting that the introduction of filming the swing had the potential to reduce the national handicap average by up to 5 strokes over its first five years of use.

Pirie's tenure was a productive one right up to the end, and during his final annual meeting as president, he supported a proposal to develop a business and merchandising committee. One of the initial concepts for the newly formed body was to set up a series of schools in sectional centers to educate members in salesmanship, with the first PGA Business Conference being held in June 1931 in Columbus, Ohio. The event focused on recruiting assistant professionals to attend the sessions, as there was a rising sentiment that they should be properly "trained for utmost service to the clubs and credit to the pro cause" and that an improved process should be in place to provide that training.

With its founding in 1916, the PGA could not have come into being at a more difficult or chaotic time. Its early professionals did not have an easy go of it. For starters, there was World War I, which forced the cancelation of tournaments everywhere and so occupied Americans once they entered the fight in the spring of 1917 that quaint recreations like golf seemed trifling and were all but ignored. Clubs closed. New course construction stopped, and old tracks sometimes went to seed. Players stopped playing, and professionals stopped teaching. It was a dismal time for the sport.

To be sure, the end of the War to End All Wars in 1918 brought relief to the U.S. golf community, as did the era of financial growth and gain that came to be known as the Roaring Twenties. That also turned out to be a prosperous time for golf, with the total number of U.S. courses tripling

from 1916 to 1923 to more than 1,900, and then soaring to just under 5,900 by 1930. Much of that growth was in public courses, as duffers all over the country found inspiration in Francis Ouimet's stirring win in the 1913 U.S. Open at Brookline and started to play the game more. In addition, nongolfers suddenly found reason to pick it up themselves. There was also a rush to construct elegant private clubs, and massive new facilities like Olympia Fields and Medinah in Chicago came into being. Things, to put it mildly, looked very good.

Disaster came again, though, this time in the form of the crash of the American stock market in the fall of 1929 and the eventual onset of the Great Depression. Any and all momentum that golf had acquired after World War I was stifled by the very harsh economic realities of that era.

Still, the game continued to be bolstered by the influx of immigrant and homebred professionals who chose to make their living in the game. Jim Barnes, an Englishman who was only 20 years old when he left his native Cornwall for the New World in 1906, was one such professional. Known as Long Jim as a result of his being six-foot four, he had been laboring as an apprentice club-maker and assistant professional at West Cornwall Golf Club when he moved to the United States. Upon his arrival, he headed immediately for the West Coast, taking a job as a teaching professional under Scotsman George Smith at Claremont Country Club in Oakland, California, before moving first to the Spokane Country Club in Washington and then the Tacoma Country and Golf Club. In 1914, Long Jim headed back East, to accept a position at the Whitemarsh Valley Country Club in Philadelphia, quickly establishing himself as one of the most formidable golfers in the game. In time, he came to be regarded as the

OPPOSITE Robert White was the first president of the PGA of America, a founding member of the American Society of Golf Course Architects, and helped put Myrtle Beach, South Carolina, on the map as a top golf destination.

first dominant player in the Association's first generation of professionals.

Winning the 1914 Western Open, which was then regarded as a major on the professional tour in America, was a good first step to earning that acclaim. Finishing in the top 20 of four consecutive U.S. Opens, from 1912 to 1915, furthered it. What really secured Barnes's position at the top of the golfing heap, however, were his triumphs in the first two PGA Championships. The inaugural event was conducted at the Siwanoy Country Club outside of New York City in 1916, with Barnes prevailing over Jock Hutchison in the finals of what was then a match play competition. Three years later, Long Jim won again, when the PGA staged its second Championship after taking two years off during World War I. This time, he thrashed Fred McLeod to once again take possession of the Wanamaker Trophy, 6 and 5. Those were impressive victories, to be sure. Barnes then did himself one better by coming out on top in the 1921 U.S. Open.

The National Championship was held in late July that year at Columbia Country Club in Chevy Chase, Maryland, just outside Washington, DC. Barnes arrived at the site only a day before the competition began. In recalling the event years later, he said: "I went into the Open fresh. I led the qualifying with a 69 that broke the course record the first time I saw the whole course. Then I shot another 69 on the first round and led all the rest of the way." He said this in his typically humble manner, for he not only led the rest of the way but also demolished the field in the process, winning by 9 shots over Walter Hagen and host professional McLeod and 14 strokes ahead of fourth-place finisher, the future Hall of Fame amateur Chick Evans.

President Warren Harding joined a gallery estimated as high as 12,000 for the final round. An avid golfer who had played a casual match with Barnes at a Florida club the year before, Harding presented the U.S. Open trophy to Barnes with the words "Congratulations, partner."

Four years later, Barnes captured his last major, winning the 1925 Open Championship at Prestwick in West Scotland and cemented his reputation as one of the great golfers of the early 20th century. His playing garnered Barnes most of the praise and attention, but he was also highly regarded for the ways he served his members at the various clubs that employed him over the years. He helped Philadelphia businessman Spencer Penrose open the Broadmoor in Colorado Springs in 1918 and held the head professional's position there for a year. After that, Barnes moved to the Sunset Country Club in St. Louis, and then returned to the metropolitan New York area, with stints at some of its finest retreats, such as Essex Country Club in New Jersey and the North Hempstead Country Club in Long Island. Along the way, Barnes also managed to produce what historians regard it as the first detailed photographic study of the swing. Titled *Picture Analysis of Golf Strokes: A Complete Book of Instruction*, it featured more than 300 photographs of Barnes swinging a golf club.

Carnoustie gave the States another of its golf-savvy native sons when George Low emigrated in the spring of 1899 to assume the position of head professional at the Dyker Meadow Golf Club in Brooklyn. It marked the beginning of a long and fruitful career for Low, who gained his greatest repute as the professional at the esteemed Baltusrol Golf Club in Springfield, New Jersey, from 1903 to 1925. In addition, his presence gave the fledging American golf scene one more master from which it could learn about the increasingly popular sport.

While Low was best known for his work as a club professional, he also distinguished himself as a competitive player, twice finishing in the top six of the U.S. Open. He gained acclaim as a deft course architect and is credited with designing and building the nation's first-ever island green, on the 10th hole on the original Long Course at Baltusrol. Low also opened an off-course retail store in New York City and created the famed furrowed bunker rake that was used to maintain the sandy hazards at the Oakmont Country Club. He was a skilled club-maker and a big personality who instantly made his members and their guests feel comfortable.

Though Dyker Meadow was the job that brought Low to the States, it was not the only place he worked after he first crossed the Atlantic. He traveled to Florida in the winters, to teach and also to play, and to Vermont in the summers, to serve members at the bucolic Ekwanok Country Club in Manchester. At the same time, Low continued to oversee operations at Dyker. Then, in 1903, he took the professional's position at Baltusrol, which was getting ready to host its first U.S. Open, and assumed the job of greenkeeper there as well.

Low labored happily at Baltusrol for the next 23 years, leaving not long after the club had made him a lifetime member. He traveled back home to Carnoustie with every intention to retire, but then the stock market crash of 1929 wiped out his investments, forcing him to go back to work. So, Low returned to the States, to take over as professional at the Huntingdon Valley Country Club near Philadelphia. He also founded an enterprise called "George Low's Driving Range" in Flourtown, Pennsylvania. In those positions, Low wowed the good people of Philadelphia, so much so that the PGA Section there named him an honorary Section president for his many contributions. Retirement may have been a more pleasurable alternative for the Scotsman, but he made the best of a less than optimal situation and once again made his mark in American golf.

In the February 1948 issue of *Professional Golfer Magazine*, H. J. Chapman's article "Ghosts of Carnoustie" highlighted how the "little Scottish town of 4,000 folk" sent more than 300 professionals to the United States in the early years of the game in this land. Among the most impressive and talented of them all, he acknowledged, was George Low.

Women were not allowed to be members of the PGA at its founding in 1916, however that did not deter a foursome of females from making a living in the game as golf professionals when the Association was just coming into being. In fact, those ladies not only served as evangelists of the sport in its early years in America but also as pioneers who blazed the trail that so many women would eventually follow.

Georgina Campbell from Musselburgh, Scotland, is regarded as the first woman professional in America. She emigrated to the States with her husband, Willie Campbell, in 1894, when he became head professional at The Country Club in Brookline, Massachusetts, and also the nearby Essex Country Club. Later, he moved to the Myopia Hunt Club just north of Boston, and his workload became so great that he brought in Georgina to help in his pro shop. She was a skilled club- and ball-maker as well as a strong teacher and merchandiser, and she lent a very welcome hand. When Willie died in 1900, after they had helped found and then run the Franklin Park public golf facility in Boston, Georgina succeeded him as golf professional.

Isabella May Gourlay Dunn was another groundbreaker. She, too, hailed from Musselburgh, and her uncle was the famed golf professional Willie Dunn Jr. After arriving in the States in 1915, she moved to Lake Tahoe, Nevada, where she designed a 6-hole course with sand greens for the internationally famous Tahoe Tavern resort. The owners retained her as the golf professional once the course was completed,

The Turnesa family of Elmsford, New York, produced seven brothers who became PGA Professionals that competed at the highest level, including, *left to right*, Joe, Mike, and Jim.

and she acquired the nickname Queenie. During the 1940s and 1950s, the Tahoe Tavern served as the site of many big-money games that involved entertainers like Bing Crosby, Bob Hope, Frank Sinatra, and Dean Martin, as well as top amateurs Ken Venturi and Harvie Ward along with their patron Eddie Lowery, who at age 10 was Francis Ouimet's caddie in the 1913 U.S. Open and later became a successful San Francisco auto dealer.

Unfortunately, Dunn's professional career was short-lived. According to an announcement in *The Troy Times*, dated January 18, 1923: "America's Only Professional Woman Golfer, Mrs. May Isabella Gourley Dunn-Webb, found romance on the greens, and now she's wife of Adolph Glaser Hupfel, whom she married in San Francisco. After the honeymoon they will live in New York." They did move to New York, which is where Dunn died in 1948, at the age of 68.

In addition to Campbell and Dunn, the first decades of the 20th century also saw the emergence of homebred women professionals, and the most notable of those were Bessie Fenn and Helen MacDonald. Fenn, whose golf professional father, Arthur Harris Fenn, introduced her to the game, served for many years in that position at the exclusive Palm Beach Golf Club in Florida, while MacDonald came into the sport by working with her golf professional husband, Bob, at an indoor golf school that they ran in Chicago.

Bessie Fenn took up golf when she was seven years old and got good in a hurry, frequently competing in amateur tournaments in Florida and Maine, where her father held seasonal jobs. In time, she became good enough to compete in four U.S. Women's Amateurs.

Though she was trained to be a nurse, Fenn made golf her life. She was often at her father's side, playing and teaching with him, and when he died unexpectedly in the spring of 1925, she succeeded him as head professional at the Palm Beach Golf Club, where he had been working in the winter months. Despite the relationship, there was no sign of nepotism here, as she was chosen from a pool of more than 400 applicants.

In Fenn's day, the Donald Ross–designed course at her Palm Beach club was filled with the rich and famous, and she dealt with them brilliantly. One well-told story has Fenn chasing the golf-loving Duke of Windsor down the first fairway, shouting after him: "Dooook! Doook! You forgot to pay your green fee!" A traditionalist when it came to walking, Fenn was against the introduction and use of golf carts, unless they were needed by those with medical conditions. Members lauded her for her strong management skills as well as her teaching aptitude, and for many years she held the women's course record.

Fenn relished her work at the Palm Beach club, which is now known as Palm Beach Country Club, staying there until she retired in 1959, at the age of 70. Hers was a golf life well led, and her only real regret came when the all-male PGA of America rejected an application she made for membership, declining to change their policy at the time and allow for female professionals even though she was recognized as being the first homebred female to head up a major club operation.

When Helen Bruhn Pemberton married Robert (Bob) MacDonald in 1924, she knew she was marrying one of America's leading golf professionals. What she may not have realized, however, was that through that union, she would develop into one herself.

A native of Dornoch, Scotland, Bob MacDonald moved to the States in 1911. Six years later, he relocated to the Chicago area, taking a job first at the Indian Hill Club before moving

to the Evanston Golf Club in 1919 and then Bob O'Link Golf Club. His teaching was widely praised, and he was a strong tournament golfer as well, winning the Florida, Metropolitan, and Texas Opens, among other events. In 1924, he married a recently divorced socialite, Helen Bruhn Pemberton, and the two began traveling around the country together to tournaments and golf events. At the time, MacDonald also ran an indoor golf school in Chicago with fellow professional Jock Hutchison, and MacDonald's wife, Helen, soon began teaching with him. A few years later, MacDonald went out on his own, opening a 20,000-square-foot center called Bob MacDonald's Golf School on the sixth floor of the Leiter Building in the Loop. It boasted an 18-hole putting course as well as 12 netted hitting stations.

Records suggested that Helen turned professional when she began teaching students indoors alongside her husband in 1924. While their marriage lasted only six years, she gave MacDonald credit for bringing her into the game. She also continued to make a living at it even after they split up, founding her own indoor golf school in Chicago's Loop. In time, she came to be called "The Dean of Women Golf Teachers," and it is estimated that she taught more than 30,000 students during a career that came to a close when she shuttered her school in the mid-1960s. Perhaps no one spoke so clearly of her talents as an instructor than fellow Chicago-area professional and former PGA of America president Alex Pirie, who after watching her conduct a clinic stated: "I regard Helen MacDonald's work here this morning as one of the finest demonstrations of ability to impart golfing knowledge to beginners that I have ever witnessed. Her uncanny ability to hold the women and girls here at so high a pitch of genuine interest in everything she is showing them is almost unbelievable. Golf would be

better off were there more Helen MacDonalds."

The story of this celebrated clan that became so associated with golf and the PGA begins in 1875 with the birth of Vitale Turnesa in a small village east of Salerno, Italy. Orphaned as a youngster, he labored as a shepherd in the Italian countryside until he was able to save enough money to pay for passage to the United States. Finally, when he was 14 years old, he could afford to make the trip.

Shortly after arriving in New York, Turnesa established residence on the Lower East Side in Manhattan's Little Italy, the city's poorest neighborhood. He found a job as a shoeshine boy and quickly worked his way up to a steward position on a fleet of ferryboats run by the Erie Lackawanna Railroad. Turnesa also met, and then married, Anna Pascarella and shortly thereafter began a family that would eventually include seven sons and two daughters.

Family legend has it that one day in 1908, Vitale set out on foot from Manhattan to Westchester County to see where a relative had purchased some land. Twenty-six miles into his walk, he came upon a worksite in the countryside of Elmsford where laborers were digging into the ground with picks and shovels. Drawn to the wooded area, he applied successfully for a job to work on a crew building a new 9-hole layout for Fairview Country Club. Once construction was completed, Turnesa joined the maintenance staff, eventually becoming foreman and then the golf course superintendent. He ended up working at Fairview for 52 years, retiring when he was 80 years old.

In the beginning, the young Turnesa family lived locally with relatives. This gave them the opportunity to save for a home of their own, which Vitale eventually built with his own hands and with the help of relatives and friends. It was located less than a mile from the club.

Not surprisingly given their father's occupation and their proximity to Fairview, all seven Turnesa sons gravitated to the game of golf, with six of them serving for most of their adult lives as PGA Professionals.

Phil was the oldest of the Turnesa brothers, and he worked for 50 years as the head professional at the Elmwood Country Club in Westchester County, managing to capture one PGA Tour title, in 1932, and overseeing golf course maintenance as the greenkeeper.

Next in line was Frank, and while he toyed with the idea of becoming a doctor, he, too, made his career as a golf professional at three clubs in the New York area, among them Metropolis and Briar Hills. A natural leader, Frank always headed up family meetings, of which there were many.

Over six feet tall, Joe was the tallest of the seven golfing brothers and also the most prolific champion, earning 15 official PGA Tour titles. He played out of Elmwood as its "touring professional" and was also a member of two Ryder Cup teams. Joe twice came close to winning majors, finishing second to Bobby Jones in the 1926 U.S. Open, and then losing in the finals of the PGA that same year to Walter Hagen. While Elmwood was where Joe hung his professional's hat for much of his competitive career, he also played out of several other clubs, most of which were in the New York area, such as Bedford Hills, Alpine Country Club, and Rockville Links.

Mike was brother No. 4. He held two assistant's positions, one at Metropolis and the other at Inwood Country Club in Long Island, before being named playing professional at Fairview in 1931. While competing on tour, Mike discovered that he preferred a road less traveled so he decided to spend a majority of his career as a home professional, in his case at the Knollwood Country Club in his hometown of Elmsford.

He started there in 1943 and remained at the retreat until his retirement 44 years later.

Even though he did not love being a touring professional, Mike still found a way to win six official PGA Tour titles. He also came very close to taking the 1948 PGA Championship at Norwood Hills Country Club in St. Louis. After making it to match play, he fought his way to the finals, needing 37 holes to beat reigning Masters champion Claude Harmon in the semis. His next opponent was Ben Hogan, and true to form the Hawk bore down, beating Mike in the 36-hole match by a score of 7 and 6.

Though Mike impressed many with his tournament play, it is as a club professional at Knollwood that he is best remembered. In 1963, the Metropolitan PGA Section recognized him as its Golf Professional of the Year, and in 1986 it gave him the Sam Snead Award in recognition of his contributions to golf and the PGA. After he passed away in October 2000, Mike was laid to rest wearing his green Knollwood blazer with a rosary wrapped in his hands.

Like older brothers Phil and Frank, fifth brother Doug Turnesa concentrated his career on being a club professional. He was a physically strong individual, but had no interest in playing on the PGA Tour. He simply loved being at his club, where he concentrated on teaching and merchandising, serving the Briar Hall Country Club in Briarcliff Manor, New York, as its professional for 24 years.

The sixth of the Turnesa brothers was Jim, and he was born in 1912, the same year as Ben Hogan, Byron Nelson, and Sam Snead. This Turnesa also developed into a strong player, wining a number of titles on and off the PGA Tour, including the 1946 Westchester PGA Championship, the 1947 North and South Open, the 1951 Reading Open, and the 1952 Havana Open in Cuba. He also collected the Argentine Open in 1952 on the invitation of his good friend

Paid

Mr. Herbert Strong,
    Secretary of the Organization Committee,
      Professional Golfers' Association of America,
        Inwood, Long Island, New York.

Dear Sir:
      The undersigned, a professional golfer regularly employed by a regularly constituted Golf Club, hereby makes application for membership in The Professional Golfers' Association of America as a Class "A" member, and agrees to remit $10 to the treasurer within ten days after notice of his election to membership by the Organization Committee.

      The undersigned further agrees that his signature to this application for membership shall be accepted as his formal signature to the Constitution and By-laws of the Association, binding him to agree to live up to and abide by all the rules adopted by the Association as indicated in the rough draft submitted and revised and adopted by the Organization Committee.

Dated *April 14* 1916   Signed *Walter C. Hagen*

                                        Club *Rochester Country Club*

Approved *Yes*   City *Rochester*

                                     County *Monroe*

                                         State *N. Y.*

Rejected ....   Home Street Address *R. F. # 1*

Roberto De Vicenzo and finished third in the 1948 U.S. Open, behind Jimmy Demaret and Ben Hogan. The following year, Turnesa once again finished third in the Open.

Four years later, however, Jim Turnesa ended the family's 26-year curse in the majors when he captured the 1952 PGA Championship in Louisville, Kentucky. The next year he played on the American Ryder Cup team, which faced off against the GB&I squad at the Wentworth Club outside London. In a close contest, the United States captured its sixth Ryder Cup in a row by a score of 6 1/2 to 5 1/2, with Turnesa prevailing in his only match, against Peter Alliss.

With all six of his older brothers golf professionals, it seemed only logical that Willie Turnesa would follow in their footsteps, but his brothers wanted to make sure he took a different path. It wasn't because they didn't love the game, but rather because they all wanted him to have something they never attained: a college education.

The youngest Turnesa brother came of college age in the midst of the Great Depression. Willie's brothers were surviving as golf professionals, but it was tough. To assure his brightest possible future, and fulfill their parents' dream for all their sons, the brothers combined their resources to pay Willie's way through college at Holy Cross, a Jesuit liberal arts college in Worcester, Massachusetts.

While at Holy Cross, Willie Turnesa rose to prominence as one of the country's leading amateurs. He won the New England

ABOVE Walter Hagen's approved PGA membership application. OPPOSITE Gene Sarazen, *left*, with the Wanamaker Trophy in 1922 at Oakmont Country Club, where he captured the first of three PGA Championships.

Intercollegiate Golf Association Championship three times and was a National Collegiate Athletic Association medalist twice. He also won the Westchester Amateur Tournament two times and the Metropolitan Amateur once.

Just after graduation, Willie Turnesa entered, and then captured, the U.S. Amateur at the Oakmont Country Club. Over the next nine years Turnesa grew his reputation as a great amateur, even though he served four years

during WWII in the navy where he finished as a gunnery instructor. He was a standout on the U.S. team in the 1947 Walker Cup, taking both his foursomes and singles matches. Turnesa followed that by prevailing in the 1947 British Amateur Championship played at Carnoustie. Then, in 1948, he recorded his second U.S. Amateur title. Turnesa returned to defend his British Amateur that year but lost in the semifinals. He went on to represent the United States in the 1949 Walker Cup and also to act as the playing captain in the 1951 victory at Royal Birkdale. Following that event, he began to cut back on his national competitive schedule so he could spend more time with his wife and two daughters. One can argue that Willie had the best competitive playing record of all the Turnesa brothers, but he was the only one who never played the game as a professional.

Luck and location had almost everything to do with another pair of future PGA Professionals, Hank Dettlaff and John Revolta, getting into the game. They both happened to be raised in homes that abutted a 9-hole golf course in Oshkosh, Wisconsin, and as young boys, they found summer work on that layout as caddies. Those part-time jobs turned into lifetime employment, and the two men went on to serve the game in a number of important ways.

In the latter part of the 1890s, the wealthy residents of Oshkosh decided they wanted to have a golf course, so they formed Algoma Country Club, locating it on a south shore bluff overlooking Lake Buttes des Morts. Hank Dettlaff began caddying there in 1907, when he was nine years old. One summer, he was walking close behind a horse-drawn mower when the horse suddenly pulled to a stop. Dettlaff tripped and fell into the mower blades, bracing his fall with his left arm. The spinning blades so badly mangled his arm that his doctor suggested amputating it. Dettlaff's father adamantly disagreed, worried that his working-class son might never be capable of supporting himself in adulthood. The doctor acquiesced, and though he was able to save the young man's arm, it was terribly scarred. For the rest of his life, Detlaff wore long-sleeve shirts to hide those marks.

After World War I, Oshkosh built a new municipal golf course so the public would also have a place to tee it up. Having become a good golfer in his caddie days, Dettlaff was one of

two candidates to be the course's first manager and golf professional. After performing well in an on-course interview, city leaders offered him the job. He started working on Memorial Day in 1921. The new facility with the 9-hole course was named Mary Jewell Park, and Hank Dettlaff not only gave lessons but also sold golf equipment out of the back of an old Ford pickup truck. In addition, he worked as the greenkeeper and initiated a caddie program, realizing full well what golf and that occupation had done for him and wanting to do the same for others.

The golf course, which was one of only 60 public tracks in the nation at the time, prospered with Dettlaff at the helm, so much so that in the late 1920s, he decided to hire an assistant, selecting a young caddie named Johnny Revolta who had developed a strong interest and aptitude for the game.

For 35 years, Dettlaff oversaw operations at Mary Jewell Park, which was renamed the Lakeshore Municipal Golf Course in the late 1940s. He introduced hundreds of young boys to the game of golf through his caddie program and gave Oshkosh residents a place to tee it up. He worked tirelessly to improve the layout and conditioning of the golf course and oversaw its design and expansion to an 18-hole track, thanks to money and laborers provided through several New Deal programs. The new routing was so highly regarded that the Wisconsin PGA staged its Section Championship there in 1939.

Dettlaff also took time to work on his competitive game. He became good enough to qualify for the U.S. Open and the PGA Championship in 1934 and in later years captured two regional titles as well as the Wisconsin Senior PGA Championship, but the majority of his time was spent tending to the needs of the men, women, and children who played their golf at his municipal course and to the caddies who were looping there.

Dettlaff met his future wife, a graduate nurse named Helen Wesmarovich, during a golf lesson. The couple married in the winter of 1943 and had three children, Peter, William, and Mary. Dettlaff continued to work at the golf course until the summer of 1956, when he died of a heart attack. He was only 57 years old. His passing left a void both in his young family and also in the community, which got together and had a monument erected at the course in his honor that read: "In Memory of Hank Dettlaff. Given by his golfing friends and associates."

One individual who took Dettlaff's death particularly hard was Johnny Revolta. Dettlaff had brought Revolta into golf as a caddie at Mary Jewell Park, given him his first set of clubs, made him his personal caddie whenever Dettlaff teed it up in tournaments, and hired him as his assistant professional, in 1928. By the time he took that job, Revolta was already distinguishing himself as a player, winning the individual 1925 State Caddie Championship.

Following the 1928 season at Mary Jewell Park, Revolta secured his first head professional position, at Swan Lake Country Club in Portage, Wisconsin. He moved around a lot over the next five years, taking head professional jobs at a series of smaller clubs as he also made his mark as a player. As he did, his game only got better. Revolta won the Wisconsin Open in 1930 and 1931 and then again in 1934 and 1935. By the mid-1930s, he was a regular on the PGA Tour, playing in events such as the Western Open, the PGA Championship, and the U.S. Open. In 1934, he accepted an invitation to compete in the first Masters, then known as the Augusta National Invitation Tournament. A year later, Revolta won the PGA Championship and the Western Open while earning a spot on the U.S. Ryder Cup team. Only 24 years old at the time, he also turned out to be the Tour's leading money winner. That performance on the PGA Tour

induced the leaders at Chicago's Evanston Golf Club to hire Revolta as its head professional, and he held that position until 1966, when he became professional emeritus.

Displaying the sort of versatility among PGA Professionals that was quite common in those days, Revolta distinguished himself in a number of ways. As a competitor, he amassed a total of 18 PGA Tour victories and played on a pair of Ryder Cup squads. As a teacher, he became well-known for mentoring a young amateur named Patty Berg, who ended up becoming one of the greatest female touring professionals in golf history. Revolta also came to instruct a number of other top women players, including Mickey Wright, Kathy Whitworth, and Betsy Rawls, as he also counseled PGA Tour pros like Bob Goalby, Jay Haas, and J.C. Snead. In addition, he is credited with teaching Hogan the intricacies of the waggle and the famous Hogan finish.

While Revolta did most of his teaching on the range at Evanston, he also found his way into the television studio, becoming in the process the cohost with nine-time PGA Tour winner Jimmy Hines of what is believed to be golf's first television show, *Pars, Birdies and Eagles*. Aired on WGN Television in Chicago, it was sponsored by Joe Jemsek and Charles Nash as a way of promoting their local, daily-fee courses.

When Revolta stepped down as head professional at Evanston in 1966, he also began teaching in the winters at the Mission Hills Country Club in Rancho Mirage, California. It was there that he died, in 1991, at the age of 79.

As was the case with his mentor, Johnny Revolta was honored at the place where he gave so many lessons, with the folks at Mission Hills installing a large bronze plaque on their range three years before his death. It featured his bust in relief and read: "This Practice Tee Is Dedicated to Johnny Revolta. A Great Player and Teacher."

CHAPTER

FOUR

The Great Depression and World War II

In spite of the challenges of World War I, the first generation of American PGA Professionals established a firm footing in the United States in the years after its 1916 founding, They prospered through the Roaring Twenties, but then came the stock market crash of 1929 and the financial despair of the Depression, and golf once again became very back-of-mind and a luxury that few people could afford.

Many clubs closed due to financial travails, and those that were able to stay open often cut way back on maintenance and member services. As a result, hundreds of golf professionals lost their jobs. It was a difficult development for those individuals, but some of the suddenly unemployed were able to find relief in the form of jobs created by New Deal agencies like the Works Progress Administration and the Civil Works Administration. Several of those jobs involved the construction, renovation, or expansion of 600-odd municipal golf courses around the country, including the massive Bethpage State Park project in Farmingdale, New York, where the fabled Black Course was built.

The advent of World War II did not make things any easier, as it led to the immediate cancellation of all major golf tournaments in the British Isles and continental Europe. The same thing happened in the United States after it entered the conflict in December 1941. Clubs continued to plod along as best they could, but with so many citizens serving in the military and supporting the war effort in various other ways, things on the golf scene remained sketchy at best.

The war years did produce some promising developments for the sport. During that time, for example, President Franklin Delano Roosevelt asked a man named John B. Kelly to serve as the assistant U.S. director of civilian defense in charge of physical fitness. A two-time Olympic gold medal winner in rowing who also happened to be the father of actress Grace Kelly, he saw golf as a "game for national service of vital character" and advocated it as a way for Americans to improve their mental and physical conditioning.

The PGA decided to take advantage of that initiative by working with the government as well as with private clubs and public golf facilities to implement new programs to spread the game to the masses. Statistics show that more than 200,000 servicemen were introduced to golf when practice ranges, putting greens, and golf courses were built on military bases and staffed by volunteer PGA Professionals during World War II. High-profile players and teachers took the sport to military hospitals via exhibitions and clinics introducing the game's benefits, both physical and psychological, to recovering soldiers. Coaxed into sharing his story, World War I veteran Tommy Armour talked to GIs about how he had sustained and overcome severe injuries on the battlefields of Europe, going on to become a popular winner of the British Open Championship, the U.S. Open, and the PGA Championship. Taken together, those initiatives helped introduce golf to vast segments of the public and laid a foundation for huge increases in the number of players once the war ended.

Things did improve once the war was over. An economic boom took hold in the 1950s, and that helped grow the middle class, making golf more economically feasible and accessible to the populace. It was also beneficial having Dwight D. Eisenhower in the White House, as he loved the game and was not inclined to hide his passion for it. In fact, he played some 800 rounds of golf during his eight years in office and had a putting green installed on the White House grounds. That brought great attention to the game and so did the decisions by network television executives to start airing professional tournaments on TV. Those developments gave golf a tremendous boost in popularity, and that was good news for the PGA Professional.

By the end of World War II and the beginning of the boom-boom 1950s, there was growing divide between traditional golf professionals who performed a wide range of duties for their clubs and those who devoted more of their time to playing competitively and less to working on the lesson tees and in their pro shops. At the same time, there was a transition taking place in sales in those places of business, as golf apparel became as popular as the balls and clubs that had traditionally brought in most of the revenues. PGA of America leaders began placing a greater emphasis on member education and also on instilling better business practices throughout the game. Generally speaking, those developments had a positive impact on the life of the PGA Professional, and his ranks grew, from more than 1,800 in 1936 to some 3,500 two decades later.

Among the most notable PGA Professionals of this era was George Jacobus, and for him, golf was very much a family affair. His uncle Joe Mitchell was a charter member of the PGA, and after caddying for a couple of years, Jacobus went to work for Mitchell when he assumed the head professional's position at the Ridgewood Country Club in New Jersey. Jacobus quickly learned what it took to make it in the golf business from his uncle as he also developed a deep passion for the game, turning professional the following year, when he was 17.

Jacobus worked for Mitchell for four years, and when his uncle left for a job at the nearby Montclair Golf Club, Jacobus became the new head professional at Ridgewood. The year was 1919, and some club members wondered about putting so young a man in charge of such an important golf operation, for Ridgewood was regarded as one of the finest clubs in the Garden State, It turned out to be a perfect fit, and Jacobus would end up serving as head professional there for more than 50 years.

From almost the very beginning, Jacobus was regarded as a professional's professional, and his devotion to the game as well as his versatility were hallmarks of his career. He was a fierce advocate of junior golf, for example, and thought the future of golf rested with the young players he worked so hard to bring into the game. He taught large classes of boys and girls, and he refused to charge them for his instruction, arguing that "I have more adult pupils that I can take care of, and the fees I collect from them [for lessons] and from the sale of clubs and balls repays me for the time and work I put into instruction for young people."

Jacobus also had a keen eye for talent, and he became known as a great mentor of future PGA Professionals. Perhaps his best hire came in 1935, when he induced a young Byron Nelson to be his assistant at Ridgewood. In addition, Jacobus possessed natural leadership skills, which was why his colleagues elected him president of the PGA's New Jersey Section for five years and then asked him in 1932 to serve as head of the Association's national body, making him the first homebred professional ever to hold that position. He would preside over the PGA for the next seven years, all the while holding his day job at Ridgewood.

Jacobus accomplished many things while at the helm of the PGA, including the creation, in the midst of the Great Depression, of a golf course consultant program run by his good friend and honorary Ridgewood member, A. W. Tillinghast. In Jacobus's view, the Association could create added value to the employment of PGA Professionals by offering free course consulting services by a leading architect. The idea was for Tillinghast, who had been invited to that lunch in 1916 that officially launched the PGA, to assist clubs and courses who employed PGA Professionals in finding low-cost ways to improve their facilities through streamlined designs rendering lower maintenance costs, increased pace of play, and improved revenues and greater enjoyment of the game.

Tillinghast took his work for the PGA very seriously, reporting back to Jacobus on a near-daily basis with detail of the courses he visited and specific recommendations that were made at each facility. In time, the PGA provided each club with detailed sketches for either the course staff or outside contractor to follow.

The program proved so successful the PGA extended the architect's initial two-month contract with one that lasted for two years. During that time, Tillinghast visited hundreds of golf courses across the country. One area of focus in his recommendations was the removal of thousands of unnecessary, and unnecessarily penal, bunkers that he called "Duffer's Headaches." Said Tillinghast, "I have contended that these have been maintained at considerable cost to nearly 400 clubs, that they unnecessarily harass the great majority of those who take to the game for pleasure without in the least causing that comparatively small number of par shooters to give them a thought, and usually injecting a thoroughly discordant note and smudging an otherwise beautiful picture of rural landscape."

After stepping down as president of the PGA in 1939, Jacobus once again devoted his full attention to Ridgewood. In 1962, the New Jersey Section named him its Golf Professional of the Year, and a year later Ridgewood members celebrated his 50 years of service with a black-tie dinner attended by more than 250 of his closest friends. By all accounts, it was a grand affair.

Johnny Farrell enjoyed an equally impressive career as a PGA club professional, as he also distinguished himself as a competitive player. Born of Irish immigrant parents in White Plains, New York, the dapper, good-looking young man was only 19 years old when he took his first job as head professional, at the newly opened Quaker Ridge Golf Club in Scarsdale, New York. The next year, he captured his first PGA Tour event, the 1921 Garden City Open, beginning a 13-year stretch when he played regularly on the Tour and played well. Farrell took his second Tour event in 1922 and then a third a year later. He added two more titles in 1925 and four more the following campaign. Then, in 1926, Farrell reeled off a then-record six wins in a row, including the prestigious North and South and the Met Open. Suddenly, Farrell was celebrated as one of the best in the game, but golf writers often noted that he had yet to win a national championship, making him likely to be the first golfer in America ever described as being the "best never to have won a major."

All that changed at the1928 U.S. Open, which was staged at the Olympia Fields Country Club in Chicago, and which Farrell won by a stroke in a 36-hole playoff against Bobby Jones. More than anything else, that victory made the man a celebrity, and Farrell was suddenly signing endorsement contracts for everything from golf equipment to cigarettes. He wrote an instruction booklet and played exhibitions. It was at one of those events, at the Innis Arden Club in Old Greenwich, Connecticut, that Farrell met his future wife, a young blonde socialite named Kay Hush, who was selling programs in the gallery. Apparently, Hush had caught his eye, and at one point during the round, he hit a suspiciously errant shot that traveled well off-line and into the crowd, rolling to a stop at the feet of that young lady. Just 19 years old, she was a decade younger than the 29-year-old champion. A quick conversation ensued, and the two began seeing each other. A year later, they married, at the nearby Siwanoy Country Club, coincidentally where Farrell had worked as a caddie master during the first PGA Championship in 1916.

In time, they became something of a celebrity couple, moving comfortably among the likes of boxer Jack Dempsey, actor Douglas Fairbanks Jr.,

and musician George Gershwin, a 10-handicap member at Quaker Ridge, where Farrell still held the head professional's job. It was said that Gershwin would often sing and play his "Rhapsody in Blue" for Kay at parties. Another sports celebrity, Babe Ruth, is reported to have given her a jade necklace on her 21st birthday.

For the first few years of marriage, Kay Farrell accompanied her husband to tournaments, but that lifestyle changed dramatically in the spring of 1934 when Johnny Farrell left Quaker Ridge for the head job at the prestigious Baltusrol Golf Club in New Jersey. That move not only signified a change of occupation but also a transition from a heavy playing schedule to one that primarily involved the servicing of his new members. In addition, the new position provided Farrell with much-appreciated job security at a time of great economic uncertainty. It also allowed him and his wife, Kay, to start a family, and over the next decade they welcomed five children into the home, three boys and two girls. The boys would develop into outstanding players, with two of them, Jimmy and Billy, becoming PGA golf professionals.

Farrell was the golf professional at Baltusrol for 38 years, retiring in 1972. He never once gave the impression that he regretted leaving the life of a touring professional behind, even though he was quite proud of the record he amassed in his competitive years: winner of 22 PGA Tour events, a U.S. Open Championship, and a place on three different Ryder Cup teams. In fact, he embraced his job at Baltusrol, as a genial host to members and their guests, as a first-rate instructor, and as a top merchandiser, and in the process enjoyed one of the greatest second acts in golf.

OPPOSITE Johnny Farrell won the 1928 U.S. Open in historic fashion by defeating Bobby Jones in a 36-hole playoff, then later worked for 38 years as the head PGA Professional at Baltusrol Golf Club in Springfield, New Jersey.

As was the case with Johnny Farrell, Horton Smith first made a name for himself in golf as a tournament player, winning the first and third Masters ever played, as well as 30 other titles. He was also named to five consecutive Ryder Cup squads. Later in life he transitioned quite easily into the role of club professional and then became a tireless advocate for the PGA of America and the education of its constituents, serving as the Association's president from 1952 to 1954.

Born in Springfield, Missouri, in the spring of 1908, Smith came into golf as a caddie when he was only 11 years old. He became so hooked on the game that he often played in the morning before school and then caddied once classes were done. After graduating from high school, Smith entered State Teachers' College, but the call of the game began to get to him, and he left college to begin working full-time as a caddie master at the Springfield Country Club. In time, Smith became an assistant professional there and in 1927 took his first head job, at the Sedalia Country Club near Kansas City. The next year, he moved to the Oak Hill Golf Club in Joplin, Missouri, and from there he began playing on the tour.

Smith got off to a very strong start, winning two official PGA Tour events in 1928, then eight more in 1929 and an additional four in 1930. In addition to collecting a total of 32 professional wins in his career, the Joplin Ghost, as he was affectionately known, finished second a remarkable 37 times. He also accumulated a total of 16 top-10 finishes in the four majors, including those two wins at Augusta, in 1934 and 1936.

Two years before Smith captured his first Masters, he had moved to Chicago to work at the Oak Park Country Club. That signified the beginning of his evolution from tournament star to club professional, and he began cutting back on his travel schedule, playing only summer majors and some off-season events. At the same time, he began to get more involved in local association operations, eventually rising to Section president.

After serving in the Army Air Corps during World War II, Smith took a job as head professional at the Detroit Golf Club. Then, in 1950, PGA members elected him national secretary of the Association. That position gave Smith lots of exposure and recognition, and in 1952, the PGA named him its president.

Now in charge, with the ability to name chairmen and committee members, Smith shook up the PGA's organization and operations at its roots. He made sure the people named to committees, as members or chairmen, were cognizant that those were not honorary positions, and that they were expected to work. He pushed for better development and utilization of education for PGA members, especially up-and-coming assistants, and believed that the PGA, its members, and the business of golf would all benefit from having better trained and more highly educated club professionals.

Leaders at the PGA of America eventually recognized all that Smith meant to the organization in the education realm and created the Horton Smith Award. It is given on a national basis and also awarded in individual Sections, to celebrate the 37-year PGA of

OPPOSITE Two-time PGA Champion Denny Shute, *left*, and two-time Masters champion Horton Smith met in an exhibition match during World War II to aid the U.S. drive for war bonds.

America member and remember all the great work he did in golf administration and for his fellow golf professionals.

Among his fellow golf professionals during this time were Ben Hogan and Byron Nelson. While they will always be best known for their Hall of Fame playing careers, as well as for the 14 major championships they collectively won, they also deserve recognition for being longtime members of the PGA of America and for ably serving several clubs as home professionals as they competed at the highest levels of the game. To perform just one of those tasks well was commendable enough, but to excel at them both demonstrated remarkable skill and talent, and Hogan and Nelson were among a select group of PGA members who were able to manage that. In addition, the two Texans who were born months apart in 1912 merit attention for being among those second-generation PGA Professionals who gravitated toward tournament golf as their primary source of income and for better or worse instigated a separation in the Association between touring professionals and home club professionals that would only grow in years to come.

Born the son of a blacksmith in Dublin, Texas, Ben Hogan started caddying at the Glen Garden Country Club outside Fort Worth when he was 12 years old, often walking nearly 13 miles a day to and from the 9-hole course to work. Occasionally, he slept in a bunker on the golf course so he could be sure to be first in line for loops the following morning. In time, Hogan worked his way into the golf shop, where he cleaned clubs and performed other tasks. He also became an accomplished player, dropping out of high school and going professional in 1930, when he was only 17 years old.

Hogan's early years on tour were, to say the least, unsuccessful, and he relied on work as a club professional to pay the bills. He labored for a spell at the Nolan River Country Club in Cleburne, Texas, and then became the teaching professional at the tony Century Country Club in Westchester County, New York. Hogan stayed there for three years, through the 1940 season, somehow managing to win five tour events while also spending long hours on the lesson tee. Some have speculated that those days at Century are what piqued Hogan's interest and study of the golf swing, which led to the publishing in 1957 of his breakthrough book *Five Lessons: The Modern Fundamentals of Golf*. It is also interesting to note that the last year Hogan worked at Century, he also managed to top the PGA Tour money list, taking in a then-formidable $10,303.

Even as he prospered as a tour player, Hogan decided to take another club professional position, and in 1941, he moved to the Hershey Country Club in Pennsylvania. Owned by the candy magnate Milton Hershey, it was the venue for an annual Four-Ball tournament, and Hogan's primary job was to represent the club and the growing resort complex in Hershey as well as the famed chocolate bar of the same name and to make occasional appearances on behalf of the company. He held that position for 10 years, until 1951, during which time he captured six of his major championships, including the U.S. Open in 1948, 1950, and 1951; the Masters in 1951; and the 1946 and 1948 PGA Championships.

Like his good friend Ben Hogan, Byron Nelson learned about the game of golf as a caddie at the Glen Garden Country Club, and the two actually faced off against each other for the first time at a caddie tournament at that retreat in

1927, when they were both 15 years old, with Nelson winning by a single stroke in a playoff. As was the case with Hogan, Nelson moved from the caddie yard to the golf shop, where his primary duties were keeping the members' clubs clean and repairing them when need be. By the time he was 18 years old, Nelson was teeing it in amateur tournaments and playing well enough to qualify for the 1931 U.S. Amateur. Then, when he was 20, and after he lost his job as a clerk at the Fort Worth and Denver City Railway, he decided to turn professional. Nelson played the PGA Tour exclusively for one year, and then he accepted the position of head professional at the Texarkana Country Club. It gave him the opportunity to enjoy a bit of financial security and he could also continue to compete.

Nelson's likable personality and quality game quickly won favor among the club's members as well as one local girl named Louise Shofner, whom he had met at Bible study. Their relationship quickly progressed to their simple wedding in the bride's home in June of the following year. Prior to the wedding, Nelson had qualified for and played in his first U.S. Open, the 1934 edition at Merion, Pennsylvania.

In 1935, Nelson accepted a job as assistant professional to George Jacobus at the Ridgewood Country Club in New Jersey. It was a big move for the native Texan, but he recognized, as had Hogan, that the most sought-after head professional candidates came from the road that passed through the Northeast, which was the established training ground for outstanding club professionals.

While working his summer at Ridgewood, Nelson captured his first important professional title, the New Jersey State Open. A year later, he took the prestigious Met Open. First-place prize money for that win was $500, and that meant the world to Nelson, for he had a budget of only 25 cents per day for lunch and could not afford to eat in the clubhouse. He consumed a hot dog and a soda from an outside concession stand instead.

At Ridgewood, Nelson split his time between competing in the PGA Tour events and working members on the lesson tee and behind the counter in the club's golf shop. In April of 1937, he moved on, accepting the head professional position at Pennsylvania's Reading Country Club, starting there right after he had won his first Masters. He was 25 years old, and he used all $1,500 of his winner's purse to stock his new pro shop. A couple of months later, Nelson competed as part of the American team in the Ryder Cup at the Southport and Ainsdale Golf Club in England.

Nelson stayed for three seasons at Reading, and while there, he took his only U.S. Open title, in 1939. From there, he relocated to Toledo, Ohio, assuming the head professional position at the celebrated Inverness Club. He was lauded for his extraordinarily well-stocked pro shop and for giving lessons when he was not competing on tour. He also made a habit of playing with Inverness members on weekends. Remarkably, Nelson found a way to excel at both jobs, keeping his club clientele happy as he triumphed in 17 PGA Tour events, including his first PGA Championship in 1940 and a second Masters win, in a playoff against his old friend Ben Hogan in 1942.

As much as he had enjoyed his time at Inverness, and at Reading, Ridgewood, and Texarkana before, Nelson made a decision after the 1944 season to concentrate fully on his tournament golf. It was the club world's loss, to

OPPOSITE Byron Nelson was an assistant professional at Ridgewood Country Club near Paramus, New Jersey, in 1935; his wages were not enough to pay for lunch in the clubhouse, so he got by on 25 cents daily for a hot dog and soda—while winning his first big tournament, the Met Open.

Ben Hogan, *right*, defeated Mike Turnesa, *left*, by a score of 7 and 6 to win the 1948 PGA Championship at Norwood Hills Country Club near St. Louis. Hogan was 35-under-par over the 213 holes he played.

be sure, and the PGA Tour's gain, for Nelson proceeded to go on a historic tear as a full-time touring pro in 1945, winning 18 events and at one point recording a remarkable 11 victories in a row.

Golf came early to Tom LoPresti, and the Daly City, California native was drawn hard to the sport as a young boy. Over time, he learned that he did not have the tools to be a touring professional, but he loved being around golf and quickly found a way to make a living at it. LoPresti was only eight years old when he first started standing outside the fence at Ingleside Country Club waiting for balls to fly out of bounds, either selling them back to players or keeping them for his own practice. He soon began caddying at Ingleside, but then was fired for practicing on the course. He moved on to caddie at the Olympic Club and Lake Merced Country Club but was canned at both those spots for, once again, practicing on club property. At age 14, LoPresti was a credentialed caddie at San Francisco Golf Club, and after quitting school the following year, moved to the Monterey resort area, securing a job at the Del Monte Golf Course, wiping, sanding, and shellacking up to 100 sets of clubs every weekend. Some years later, a visiting professional from Sacramento's prestigious Del Paso Country Club, Frank Minch Sr., offered him the job of caddie master at his retreat. For the young teen, that marked the beginning of a 67-year career in the golf business in the Sacramento area.

LoPresti possessed a bright and entertaining personality that quickly endeared him to Minch and the Del Paso members. He advanced to a teaching assistant, remaining with the club for five seasons before becoming the head professional of the Sacramento Municipal Course, which was designed by the great Alister MacKenzie and is today part of the highly regarded Haggin Oaks Golf Complex.

Already known for his engaging and outgoing personality, LoPresti started to become recognized for his skills as an instructor. He also developed a reputation for the deft ways he promoted the game. Among his first steps at the new facility, for example, was to form the Sacramento Junior Girls Golf Club and the Sacramento Business Women's Golf Club, which are believed to be among the first of their kind in the United States. Shortly after that, he inaugurated the Sacramento Junior Boys Club, and those forward-thinking actions cemented his stature as one of the early West Coast pioneers of junior and women's golf.

For a time, LoPresti had designs to making it as a touring professional, but he simply did not have the psychological makeup to handle the pressure of competitive play. His friend Sam Snead noticed that and once remarked to LoPresti, "Because of your nerves, why don't you stick to counting money at the golf course instead of counting strokes on tour." Another colleague, Gene Sarazen, saw the same thing. "Tom, with your jumpy nerves, you don't have a chance. Why don't you do what you really excel in: be a top club professional and a public relations man. At present, your job is small, but stay here and grow with the club and the community, and I'm sure you will be a success." Taking heed of those thoughtful comments, LoPresti stuck to being a club professional, and the game of golf was better for it. He served the golfers who came to Haggin Oaks well and became a major force in the PGA, sitting on the Northern California Section Executive Board four different times and as the Section's tournament director for a number of years. He was also host professional for the 1963 USGA National Public Links Championship.

LoPresti also prospered as an instructor, and two of his students went on to excel as players. One was Bob Lunn, who captured the Publinx at Haggin Oaks in 1963 as an amateur and went on to win six times on the PGA Tour as a professional, and the other was Barbara Romack, who played on the LPGA circuit after enjoying a successful amateur career that included taking the 1954 U.S. Women's Amateur and playing on three Curtis Cup teams.

LoPresti was also known for training outstanding assistant professionals, and more than 50 of his hires over the years went on to become head professionals in their own rights. One of those was a local high school player, who began as a caddie at Del Paso Country Club and then came to Haggin Oaks as a part-time starter. His name was Ken Morton Sr., and once he was finished with college, he stayed on to become an assistant golf professional at Haggin Oaks. In time, LoPresti asked Morton to assume the title and role of co-head professional, and so began a 20-year business partnership during which they developed what is regarded today as a model public golf operation in America.

The PGA of America named LoPresti its Golf Professional of the Year in 1962. In 1994, 32 years later, he announced his retirement from Haggin Oaks. Three years after that, he passed away. In 2005, the PGA inducted him posthumously into its Golf Professional Hall of Fame, in a class that included his one-time protégé and eventual successor Ken Morton.

No accounting of golf in this period is complete without telling the story of Bill Powell. Growing up in Minerva, Ohio, a town near Canton where his father had moved the family to find work in a pottery factory, Powell began caddying when he was nine years old at a golf course called Edgewater that had opened seven miles from his house. His devotion to his work quickly earned the respect of caddie master Glen Lautzenheiser, and he took to assigning Powell to odd jobs that included simple club repair and minor course maintenance duties. The youngster also began to play the game with some dexterity and in

high school formed a golf team on which he would serve as both captain and coach.

It wasn't until Powell was encouraged by a number of adult golfers to enter his first junior tournament that he faced what would become a lifelong challenge in the game: racial discrimination. After hitchhiking 21 miles to an area tournament, golf bag over his shoulder, he arrived at the private Orchard Hills Country Club ready to enter the competition, much to the chagrin of tournament organizers, who didn't know how to handle his unanticipated appearance. "I stood around for two hours waiting for them to decide if I could play in their tournament," Powell recalled. "They didn't want me to play, but on the other hand, they knew I was a good player and popular in the area."

After leading the tournament on the final day with only a handful of holes to play, he faltered when an approach shot nicked a tree branch and settled into deep rough. Several swings and putts later, he walked off the green with an 8. Devastated with that outcome, he nonetheless continued to grind, finishing a respectable though disappointing third. "I left quietly, hitchhiking 21 of the longest miles of my life back home," he said.

Powell credited an experience in grade school as a moment that changed his life forever and contributed to his later success in golf. He was 12 years old and in the sixth grade when his school's principal looked him directly in the eye and stated: "Billy, you know you are a little colored boy and you have to realize you can't do things just as good as a white boy; you have to do them better!" Powell took those words to heart and used them as an inspiration to forge a determination to be better than the best. "From that point on I became my own role model and raised my own bar," he explained.

In college, Powell played both football and golf, attending Wilberforce University, an all-black institution located in Greene County,

OPPOSITE William "Bill" Powell served his country on D-Day only to return from World War II to find he was not welcome at local golf clubs in eastern Ohio. Undeterred, in 1946 Powell became the first African-American to build, own, and operate a golf facility in the United States. ABOVE Following her father into the family business, Renee Powell was the first African-American woman elected to membership in the PGA of America, and she is one of seven women elected honorary members of the Royal and Ancient Golf Club.

Ohio. In the summer of 1940, he met a woman named Marcella Oliver, and they married only months later. They had no money for a honeymoon and lived in a rented room in the home of a single mother. The following June, their first son, William Jr., was born.

Wanting to properly provide for his family, Powell sought a position with a local factory known as the Timken Company, but he was turned away for being black. Undeterred, Powell returned day after day, pleading for a position so he could support his family. He even brought letters of recommendations from local white leaders he had caddied for at Edgewater. Finally, he was hired as a janitor, but he was drafted into the army after the Japanese bombed Pearl Harbor that December and went off to fight in Europe.

Returning to Canton after serving in the U.S. Army as a technical sergeant, Powell came home to his family and the prewar factory position at the Timken Company. Even as he toiled there, he never gave up on the dream he had had since childhood: to build and own a golf course of his own, one that would be open to all players.

Powell and his wife, Marcella, began looking for a parcel of land on which he could create his own course, and one day they came upon an advertisement in a local newspaper for a farm east of Canton. Using a loan from a pair of local black doctors and some money from Powell's older brother Berry, they were able to purchase the property. The Powells moved into the century-old farmhouse on the property in the fall of 1946, and when Bill was not working his full-time evening shift at Timken, he was working on the land to turn his vision of a golf course into a reality.

In addition to the farmhouse, the 78-acre parcel boasted two barns in need of repair, a coop full of White Rock chickens, a milking barn, a silo, and what he called a "springhouse" used to furnish drinking water. The land was graced with apple, cherry, plum, and peach trees, and there were arbors full of Concord grapes. What was lacking was indoor plumbing.

Powell walked the property frequently and envisioned a 9-hole layout. Neighbors and friends helped prepare the land, taking down fence posts, digging up old stumps, and removing rocks from the rolling terrain. Powell routed the fairways and set up the tees and greens. He carefully chose his preferred grass varieties and began by seeding the fairways. He also created his own fertilizer mix to ensure a quality grow-in. All his work, planning, and care culminated with the opening of Clearview Golf Club in April 1948.

Never satisfied, he kept tinkering to improve the layout that took full advantage of the natural terrain. Ten years into the venture, Powell bought out his partners and began expanding, purchasing an additional 50-plus acres that allowed him to grow the course to 18 holes. In 1978, his redesigned layout opened with full complement of 18 holes, offering a par-69 layout measuring 5,900 yards.

Powell's family grew to include three children. In addition to the first-born William Jr. (Billy) was Renee, who arrived in 1946, and Larry, who followed in 1952. Clearview became a family project with all the children joining in both work and play. Success was not instant, nor did it come easy, and it took years to build Powell's financial independence on the golf course. He continued working a double schedule, beginning every weekday morning at the golf course and staying until midafternoon, when he would set off to Timken for the 3 to 11 p.m. shift. Weekends were spent entirely at Clearview. Powell followed this schedule for 23 years until he finally left Timken to devote his entire life to the golf club.

During this time, Marcella was usually found in the clubhouse, performing her duties as the club and office manager. Billy grew up working at Clearview and stayed there until he moved to San Francisco following college in 1966. Tragically, he was murdered in that city in 1967. Renee had a club in her hand by age three and developed into an outstanding player who was good enough to compete on the LPGA Tour. She has spent her entire professional career championing diversity, women veterans, and youth initiatives to grow the game. In 1979, the Silvermere Golf Complex in Cobham, England, made Powell the first woman head professional in the United Kingdom, and 17 years after that, she became the first woman of color elected to membership in the PGA. Then, in 2008, St. Andrews University in Scotland awarded her an honorary doctor of laws degree. Perhaps the ultimate tribute, however, came in 2015, when the Royal and Ancient Golf Club in St. Andrews elected her one of seven honorary members, the first women ever admitted to that august association.

Her brother, Larry Powell, began playing golf when he was five and soon after was helping his father maintain the course, quickly picking up his dad's underlying philosophy of "flowing with nature instead of fighting it." Larry established a 30-year career with the U.S. Postal Service while also working at the golf course. He also became a member of the Golf Course Superintendents Association of America.

Recognition was not instant for the Powell family and their remarkable accomplishments. Locally, they earned high accolades for the quality course and friendly, welcoming atmosphere. Indebted for what golf brought to his life as a youngster, Bill Powell devoted much of his career to personally teaching at his outstanding junior programs. He was also a strong advocate for bringing women into the game, but beyond the Canton area and Ohio it took decades for the depth of his contributions to the game to reach a national audience.

After Bill Powell was inducted into the Canton Negro Old Timers' Athletic Association Hall of Fame, the Powells received their first national recognition. It came in 1992 when the National Golf Foundation named the Powells as the Jack Nicklaus Golf Family of the Year for their 46 years of contributions to the game. That same year the Dr. Martin Luther King Jr. Commission awarded Bill Powell the Cornerstone of Freedom Award. Two years later, Powell was inducted into the National Black Golf Hall of Fame. In 2009, when he was 93 years old, the PGA presented him with its Distinguished Service Award.

In August 1999, the Association made a historic announcement at the PGA Championship at Medinah Country Club that honored Powell and Clearview. "The PGA is pleased to be involved with Clearview Golf Club because of its historical and cultural significance," said then-PGA President Will Mann. "Clearview and the Powell family are inspirational examples of the entrepreneurship in the golf business." The PGA followed by initiating a plan to remodel and preserve Clearview for generations to come. Architect Michael Hurdzan offered his services free of charge to assist Powell and his son on the course renovation and lengthening. The layout was expanded by an additional 400 yards and par increased to 72. A state-of-the-art irrigation system was installed and seven new bunkers added.

In 2001, the Clearview Legacy Foundation was started to further ensure the future of the course. Legacy plans focused on the expansion of opportunities at Clearview, including construction of a teaching facility, creation of the William and Marcella Powell Museum, and expanded clubhouse facilities. That same year Clearview was granted placement on the National Register of Historic Places by the National Park Service, becoming only the 14th golf course to be granted such status.

CHAPTER

FIVE

The Baby Boom Era

This was a very different period for PGA Professionals, as they were able to operate without the burden of world war and deep financial depression for the first time in decades. In fact, the U.S. economy boomed for much of this time, especially during the presidencies of Dwight D. Eisenhower and John F. Kennedy and later that of Ronald Reagan, and Americans were devoting more of their time to leisure activities. Those factors helped make golf an increasingly popular pastime, and so did the mass introduction of television.

As more and more households purchased and installed TVs, the demand for new programming took off, and one way that broadcast executives sought to fill that need was by airing golf. They began broadcasting major tournaments, like the PGA Championship, the Masters, and the U.S. Open. They also created made-for-TV specials such as *Shell's Wonderful World of Golf.* Television executives also started paying particular attention to the charismatic, hard-charging touring professional named Arnold Palmer as well as a young Jack Nicklaus, and those things all worked to lift the exposure and popularity of golf to new heights. More and more Americans were playing and watching the game, and golf course construction soared, in both the private and public sectors.

Alas, all was not perfect, and at the start of this era, the PGA remained 100 percent white by definition of a bylaw inserted in 1934. Fortunately, the PGA removed "the Caucasian-only" clause from its Constitution in 1961, finally opening the Association to all ethnic and racial groups and joining the rest of America in addressing long-simmering civil rights issues throughout the land.

Another conflict was resolved during this period of the PGA's history when the Association formally split into two groups. On one side was the club professional, who accounted for a majority of the Association membership and sought greater support from the parent organization for expanded education, grow-the-game initiatives, and improved business opportunities. On the other was a small but close-knit group of dedicated tournament professionals who were looking for more self-governance with the intent to gain a bigger share of revenues from competitions. The first change came in 1968—an already tumultuous year rocked by the escalation of and protests against the Vietnam War—with the creation of the fully autonomous Tournament Players Division, which possessed all the built-in rights of the other territorial Sections of the PGA, including the right to manage its own affairs and to control exclusively its own Section funds. Seven years later, that group would take on a new name: the PGA Tour.

That landmark agreement served as a historical demarcation in the world of golf. Since the days of Allan Robertson in St. Andrews, there had been only one path for a professional to follow, and to succeed in that position, he needed not only to be a deft player but also to boast a variety of other skills, from being an instructor and equipment specialist to serving as a merchandiser and organizer of tournaments. Professionals had to be the experts in all aspects of the game.

The split of the PGA brought forth a new dimension to the profession, one that was highly focused on the ability to play competitive golf at the highest level. It was accessible to a select few individuals and allowed them to focus solely on tournaments. Rather than being regarded as "golf professionals," they came to be called "professional golfers."

Other changes of note took place through the years of the baby boom. In 1956, for example, the PGA relocated its headquarters from Chicago to Dunedin, Florida, with a second move taking place nine years later, to Palm Beach Gardens. This was also a time when the PGA began devoting substantial resources to its education programs, building on the foundation Horton Smith and others from the previous generation of PGA Professionals had laid. In 1955, the Association presented an optional "golf business school" for continuing education by its members. A decade after that, its leaders decided to create the new position of national education director to oversee the broader education effort. In addition, the PGA began discussing ways to have colleges add a golf curriculum for students on athletic scholarships, believing that it would encourage the students to pursue a golf career and thus benefit the profession once they graduated. As the Association prepared to celebrate its centennial years later, PGA Golf Management University Programs were being offered at 19 universities in the United States.

The baby boom era was also a time when a number of new and highly competent PGA Professionals came onto the scene. One of those with Bill Strausbaugh, who came to be known throughout the game simply as "Coach." It says a lot about a man when he is known by a nickname, and it speaks even more loudly about his stature when leaders of that industry name one of its most important awards after him. Coach was that special an individual. Growing up in the Pimlico section of Baltimore, he found his way into golf as a caddie, looping as a young man at the Bonnie View Country Club, which was located about a mile from his home. After graduating from Calvert Hall College, a Catholic college preparatory high school, he entered Loyola University, a Jesuit college in

his hometown, but World War II broke out before he could earn his degree. Strausbaugh left Loyola shortly after the bombing of Pearl Harbor when he enlisted in the U.S. Marine Corps. He served in the Pacific Theater aboard the transport ship USAT Samuel Duncan Sturgis and later the carrier USS Wasp, seeing action in four major battles.

Following the war, Strausbaugh finished his degree at Loyola. Then he began his professional golf career at the Country Club of Maryland, working as an assistant under the same Scottish professional, Andy Gibson, who had been at Bonnie View when Coach caddied there.

For 10 years, Strausbaugh served Gibson as an assistant. Then he took his first head professional position, at Fountain Head Country Club in Hagerstown, Maryland. After six seasons there, Coach returned to Baltimore to assume the head professional's position at Turf Valley. Then came what would be the last job he ever held, as head golf professional at the Columbia Country Club in Chevy Chase, Maryland. The year was 1967, and the 44-year-old Strausbaugh succeeded the only professional that Columbia had employed since its founding in 1912, Fred McLeod. Winner of the 1908 U.S. Open, McLeod was a legend in the game and his shoes were tough to fill, but Strausbaugh turned out to be the perfect replacement, and he quickly became revered for his abilities as a golf instructor and the very comprehensible ways he made his points on the lesson tee. He interacted easily with his members on and off the course and mentored his assistant professionals, many of whom, like Jim Fitzgerald and Dennis Satyshur, would go on to take top jobs at other prestigious golf clubs.

Strausbaugh's reputation as a professional soared quite high at Columbia, and his service to the PGA and his fellow Professionals only bolstered his reputation. He held a number of offices at the Section level and sat as its president from 1974 to 1976. Strausbaugh also joined the National PGA Board for a spell and worked tirelessly to promote and augment the Association's Education Program. Throughout his career, he spoke before hundreds of amateur and professional golf groups and conducted presentations in 38 of the PGA's 41 Sections. In addition, Coach traveled in the name of instruction and professional development to eight foreign countries and taught frequently at Ferris State University in Michigan, which offered one of the first college PGA Golf Management University Programs in the country, and which was so pleased with his assistance that it endowed a scholarship in his name.

That was but one of many recognitions Coach received for his talents and hard work. In 1966, he was honored as the Middle Atlantic PGA Golf Professional of the Year as well as the PGA's National Golf Professional of the Year. Perhaps not coincidentally, the Columbia Country Club hired Strausbaugh the year after he won the award. The Section appeared to be just as impressed, presenting Strausbaugh with its Horton Smith Award five times and naming him the Teacher of the Year twice. In 1979, the PGA established the Bill Strausbaugh Award, presenting it each year to a PGA Professional who has distinguished himself by mentoring fellow PGA Professionals, helping improve their employment situations, and serving his community. It is an appropriate and enduring

OPPOSITE Called the "impresario of daily-fee golf," Joe Jemsek helped bring golf to the masses in the Chicago area, and his work provided a model for growing the game nationally.

legacy for a man who devoted a lifetime to enhancing the enjoyment of the game, the Association, and the lives and livelihood of his fellow Professionals.

Another PGA Professional who prospered during this period was Joe Jemsek. He was a man with a dream, and it first came to him when he was caddying at a golf facility called Cog Hill in the Chicago suburbs. He was 15 years old, and his foursome included the three Coghill brothers, who owned what was then a 36-hole complex. One of the players asked Jemsek what he thought of the course, and he replied, "It's the most beautiful place I have ever seen, and someday, I am going to own it."

Legend has it that the three brothers howled when they heard those words, but Jemsek was the one who had the last laugh, for the one-time looper not only ended up owning those two Cog Hill layouts but also expanding that holding into a four-course complex that hosted several USGA Championships and became the home for nearly two decades of one of the most popular stops on the PGA Tour, the Western Open. Along the way, Jemsek joined the PGA and became one of its most esteemed professionals when the Association named him its Golf Professional of the Year in 1991. He was revered as "the average golfer's best friend" and grew to be so highly regarded in the Prairie State that he was part of the inaugural class of the Illinois Golf Hall of Fame.

That was quite a ride for the son of Russian immigrants who was born in 1913 and grew up in the town of Summit just outside Chicago. Like so many Americans in those days, he made his way into golf as a caddie, first at the Laramie Golf Course and later at Club Palos, sometimes hitching a predawn ride to his loops with a pie deliveryman. Jemsek was 15 years old when Cog Hill opened, and he hopped a freight train on occasion to get himself to work, as the courses there were a dozen miles from his home. Many times, the golfers for whom he caddied gave him rides home when their rounds were done.

Jemsek did well at Cog Hill, advancing to the role of assistant professional by the time he was 17 and then being named head professional at the age of 20. At that point, he had grown to be a very competitive player, qualifying that year for the 1933 Western Open, which was contested at the Olympia Fields Country Club. A year later, Jemsek burnished his reputation as a golfer by winning a long drive contest at the Chicago World's Fair.

Jemsek moved to another Chicagoland retreat in 1939. Called the St. Andrews Golf and Country Club, it had been developed a decade earlier as part of a housing development named Lakewood. Two sisters had recently inherited the complex, and they desperately needed Jemsek's expertise and experience. He proved a skilled manager, and soon made an offer to the sisters to buy the golf courses. A jitterbug champion, Jemsek had also become quite smitten with one of those lasses, who turned out to be a trained ballerina and loved to dance as much as he did. The feeling was mutual, and it was not long before the two were married.

Jemsek was an entrepreneur in the truest sense of the word. With World War II increasing in scope, Jemsek guessed that there would likely be shortages of rubber and he bought up huge stocks of golf balls from Spalding's warehouse. That ensured that he had a healthy inventory of that product even as fighting raged in Europe

---

OPPOSITE Don Padgett, the 20th president of the PGA of America, was the 1961 PGA Golf Professional of the Year and led the development of the Junior PGA Championship.

and the Pacific, and he used that supply as a way of luring golfers to his courses, offering players a free golf ball for every greens fee they purchased. It helped keep his complex in operation during the Second World War.

Once peace came, Jemsek took to other forms of marketing, traveling to local factories to solicit new players and business. He proposed twilight leagues to workers at those factories and offered free group lessons to new leagues to first secure their commitment. He also visited union halls and political groups, inducing organizations like those to hold their outings at St. Andrews for years to come.

It wasn't long before Jemsek encountered another business opportunity, and this one allowed him to turn that childhood dream into a reality. The year was 1950, and two of

the three Coghill brothers had passed away. The surviving sibling was aging and didn't have any children to inherit the family operation. Jemsek went to talk with him, and a year later, they agreed to terms. In addition to owning the golf courses on which he used to caddie as a teenager, the entrepreneurial professional now possessed the two outstanding 36-hole facilities in the Chicago suburbs.

As Jemsek had fantasized about buying Cog Hill, he had also longed to build a championship course in the Chicago area that would be open to the public. To that end, in 1963, he hired the architectural team of Dick Wilson and Joe Lee to build a third 18-hole layout at Cog Hill. Jemsek was satisfied with the finished product but still felt it was lacking as far as testing the best players in the world. As a result, he asked

OPPOSITE Claude Harmon won the 1948 Masters, but his legacy is as a premier PGA Teaching Professional and the patriarch of an accomplished teaching family with four sons that became PGA members, including Butch, Craig, and Billy, *above, second, third, and fifth from left*, who were honored in 2007 by the GWAA for contributions to golf. (Not pictured, Dick Harmon)

the designers to construct a fourth course on an adjacent piece of property. It opened in 1964 and won instant acclaim. Average golfers flocked to the new course and raved about its challenging design and strong conditioning. Then, the elite amateur and touring professionals started to come. In 1970, Cog Hill No.4 was the site of the USGA Men's Public Links Championship. Seventeen years later, it held the U.S. Women's Public Links, and in 1991 the Western Golf Association decided to make that Cog Hill course the home of the Western Open, staging that historic event there through the 2006 season. That did not mean that Cog Hill was done with the USGA, however, and in 1997 it hosted the U.S. Amateur, which future Ryder Cup team member Matt Kuchar won.

Jemsek was the first in American golf to provide high-quality golf to the average person, and by doing so, he initiated a concept in golf course development that has now been applied to every state in the union. He showed the governing bodies of the sport that public facilities could host PGA Tour events, something that no doubt contributed to the trend of places like Pebble Beach, Bethpage Park, Torrey Pines, and Chambers Bay getting major championships in later years. No one was really surprised when *Golf Magazine* named Jemsek one of the "100 Heroes of Golf" during the centennial celebration of golf in America or when the National Golf Course Owners Association created the "Jemsek Award for Golf Course Excellence that is awarded annually to this day. He deserved every recognition he received.

Golf can often be a father-and-son affair, with the patriarch passing on his knowledge of the sport to his offspring, to say nothing of his passion for the game. Such was certainly the case in the Padgett family, who also made a big impact during this era.

After getting into golf as a caddie at a 9-hole course in Indiana, Don Sr. went on to become a PGA Professional and to be named Golf Professional of the Year at both the Section and national levels before ascending to the presidency of the Association in the late 1970s. Padgett then finished his career as director of golf at Pinehurst and was one of those responsible for bringing to U.S. Open to that hallowed retreat in 1999.

As for his only child, Don II, he, too, made a living in the royal and ancient game. A strong player, he attended Indiana University on a golf scholarship and then played on the PGA Tour for three years before taking his first head professional's position, at the Woodland Country Club in Carmel, Indiana. Four years later, Padgett the Younger accepted the job as head professional at the Firestone Country Club in Akron, Ohio. Shortly after his father died, in 2003, Don II moved to Pinehurst to take on the role of president for the 2005 U.S. Open, which was returning to the Carolina Sandhills. It was a reprise of a very familiar story, in golf and in so many other walks of life. The father leads the son, and the son follows the father.

Don Padgett Sr. was born the third in a family of six children, where his three younger sisters all passed away as infants of scarlet fever. When he was 13 years old, his father died of severe burns sustained in a home explosion when he was attempting to light a gas heater for bathwater. Padgett's widowed mother was left with three sons, and each of the boys stepped up to support their mother and assist in earning the family's livelihood. One way of doing that was through caddying, and they were always sure to pass on a percentage of their earnings from each loop to their mother.

It was during his second year of caddying that Padgett started playing the game himself. Small for his age, he had to develop a strong short game to be competitive with many of the bigger caddies. Soon, he was shooting in the 70s. Padgett played golf on the high school team, but the game became of secondary concern after he enlisted in the navy following graduation in 1943. He spent most of his time in the service on the USS *Mount Olympus*, assigned to the South Pacific. When World War II ended, he returned to Indiana and took a job at the Maxwell Motor plant, an auto factory owned by Chrysler, making $1.19 an hour. Within a year he was married, and two years later, in 1949, he and his wife, Joanne, welcomed Don II into the world. The joy of parenthood was tempered by problems at work. After an employee strike shut down the plant, Don Sr. took a job as head professional at a local American Legion golf course. He was just 23 years old.

While working at the golf course, Padgett also assumed his old position at the plant when the strike finally ended. Five days a week, he toiled at the factory on the graveyard shift and then went directly to the course to begin his golf workday, often assisted in the shop by Joanne. Somehow, he managed to find a few hours of rest in the early evening before having to head back to his factory shift, which began at 10:30 p.m.

After five years of that rather arduous arrangement, Padgett moved to a private retreat called Green Hills Country Club, near the industrial town of Muncie, Indiana. His role there was typical of many small golf operations across the country, and his duties and income came from overseeing the overall golf operation, which he ran with precision and aplomb. The position may have lacked the glamour and complexity of many larger clubs found in metropolitan areas, but it allowed him to make it a family undertaking. Don II

joined his parents at the country club, working in almost every facet of the operation. Typically, the family was the first members of the club staff to arrive each morning, and the last to leave.

Green Hills kept Padgett very busy, but that did not prevent him from finding the time to serve the PGA. In time, leaders of the Indiana PGA Section approached him about running for Section president. They appreciated that he was a talented player, but what really attracted them was the deft way Padgett ran his business. Padgett served his term as Section president from 1959 to 1960, and a year after stepping down from that job, he received the Association's highest honor, that of PGA Golf Professional of the Year.

As a result of that recognition, Padgett was besieged with job offers from places with more prestige and more money. He was flattered by the interest, but he and Joanne had found a home at Green Hills, and they had no interest in leaving, so they stayed. That did not stop Padgett from taking on new positions with the PGA, however. He ran the Indiana Section as president for a second time in 1966 and again in 1969 and 1970. He also served a term as PGA District vice president. Then, in 1973, he assumed a leadership position in the national office, moving from treasurer and secretary to vice president and finally president of the PGA, a position he held from 1977 to 1978. Padgett was elected to national office from his position at Green Hills. Perhaps Padgett's greatest accomplishment as a PGA officer was overseeing the expansion of the opposing Ryder Cup team roster from being exclusively British and Irish to include players from all of Europe.

Padgett was 62 years old when he started his final job in the golf business, as the director of golf at the fabled but somewhat faded Pinehurst

The Harmon family, *standing, left to right*: Alice, Claude Jr. (Butch), Craig, Dick, Billy, Claude Sr., *seated*, Claudia and Allison.

Resort. The year was 1987, and his mission was quite simple: restore Pinehurst to its proper place in the game and bring championship play back. Not surprisingly, Padgett did just that. The resort experience slowly but surely improved, and then the tournaments started to return. First came the PGA Professional National Championship, in October 1988. Next came the U.S. Women's Amateur, and then PGA Tour Commissioner Deane Beman contacted Padgett to see if Pinehurst would be interested in hosting the Tour Championship on its No. 2 course, which it did in 1990. The success of that event led the USGA to offer the facility the 1994 U.S. Senior Open. Shortly thereafter, the Association named Pinehurst the site of the 1999 U.S. Open.

After years of preparation, the stage was set for the 1999 Open, and the tournament played out as if it were scripted, with the course delivering a memorable finish as Payne Stewart edged out Phil Mickelson after sinking the longest winning putt in U.S. Open history. Pinehurst's future as a U.S. Open venue had been sealed, and the resort was back on the map as a world-class golf destination.

Shortly after that Open, the USGA bestowed another national championship upon Pinehurst, to be held in 2005. Sadly, Don Padgett Sr. would not live to see the return of that major, passing away on May 16, 2003. His son, Don II, would be in Pinehurst for that championship, and as much more than a casual observer.

Following his father's death, Don II asked the people at Pinehurst if they would ship his father's beloved, red-leather executive chair to Firestone, where the younger Padgett was working as the director of golf. Eighteen months later, both golf professional and red leather chair would be on their way back to North Carolina after resort executives asked Padgett to assume

what would have been his father's job running the Open at Pinehurst. Don II accepted, and for a second time in six years a U.S. Open was played on the No. 2 course under Padgett family guidance. It, too, was a huge success.

Four years after that tournament, the USGA awarded Pinehurst both the 2014 U.S. Open and U.S. Women's Open, to be contested on back-to-back weeks on the No. 2 track. The never-before-attempted dual event came off without a hitch, and several months later, Don II retired. His departure brought to a close more than a quarter century of Padgett family leadership during which the Pinehurst resort was elevated once again to the pinnacle of the game, thanks in large part to a certain father and son.

Another person who stands tall in the pantheon of PGA Professionals is Eugene "Claude" Harmon Sr. As an instructor he worked extensively with Ben Hogan and taught four U.S. presidents and Morocco's King Hassan II. As a player he captured the 1948 Masters and set course records that still stand at such notable tracks as Fishers Island, Quaker Ridge, Seminole, and the East and West Courses at Winged Foot, and as a club professional he held the top job at some of America's finest and most exclusive retreats, including Seminole, Winged Foot, River Oaks in Houston, and Thunderbird in Palm Springs among them.

Claude Harmon is regarded as one of the great golf professionals the game has ever known. He is celebrated for mentoring an all-star roster of assistants, including Jackie Burke, Dave Marr, Mike Souchak, Eddie Merrins and Jack Lumpkin, as well as for bestowing upon the game of golf the gift of four highly skilled professionals in the form of his sons Claude Jr. (Butch), Craig, Dick, and Billy. Claude's sons have very proudly and capably carried on his legacy, as has a grandson, Claude Harmon III.

Born in Savannah, Georgia, and raised in Orlando, Florida, Claude Harmon Sr. was introduced to golf as a young boy and quickly became something of a prodigy. When he was 13, he played an exhibition match with Gene Sarazen and Walter Hagen—and proceeded to shoot 63. Two years later, he qualified for the U.S. Amateur. While living in Florida, the young Harmon often caddied at Dubsdread Golf Course. One of his regular loops was Ky Laffoon, an outstanding player who would collect 10 PGA Tour titles over his career. Laffoon took Harmon under his wing, eventually asking him to work with him as an assistant at his summer jobs in the Midwest and caddying for him on the PGA in the winter.

Harmon's big break came in 1941, when Winged Foot head professional Craig Wood hired him to be one of his assistants. Four years later, Wood retired, and Harmon took over. That fall, Harmon also assumed the head professional position at the Seminole Golf Club in Juno Beach, Florida, working there in the winters and then returning to suburban Westchester County for the summer season at Winged Foot. His was a remarkable feat, holding the top position at two of the most prestigious clubs in the land, and Harmon distinguished himself in both assignments, serving Seminole for the next 14 years and Winged Foot until 1978.

In his work at those places, Harmon displayed a wide range of skills. First of all, he was an extraordinarily talented player. Harmon showed that as a boy, and his playing got only more proficient as he aged. The pinnacle of Harmon's playing career came in 1948 when he won the Masters by 5 strokes. It would be the last time a club professional would win a major. He also made semifinal appearances in three PGA Championships, when the format was

still match play. Then came the 1959 U.S. Open. Playing as the host professional, Harmon put on a stellar performance, finishing 2 shots back of champion Billy Casper and tying for third place with his former Winged Foot assistant Mike Souchak. Though Harmon secured only one other official PGA Tour victory, the 1950 Miami International Four-Ball with Peter Cooper, he did take a dozen important titles in the highly competitive Metropolitan PGA Section, including six Westchester Opens, three Westchester PGA Championships, two Met PGA Championships, and one Met Open.

Harmon also shined as a teacher, believing that any successful club professional had to be a first-rate instructor and give his members something they could not find anywhere else. In addition, he worked with players of a much higher caliber, like Ben Hogan, who spent a month or more at Seminole every winter preparing for the Masters, and also tutored presidents and kings. As a club professional, Harmon was proud of the 44 assistants he coached and trained through the years. He played regularly with members and encouraged his protégés to do the same. Harmon also appreciated how important merchandising was becoming to the successful golf professional in the postwar era, and he thought that the best way to sell equipment and apparel to his members was through building personal relationships with them.

He was respected and admired by his assistants for being a great man to work for, very encouraging and yet very tough. Harmon expected certain things from them, and he let them know in no uncertain terms how well they were doing, good or bad. One of the greatest principles he passed on was his belief that it was a privilege to be a golf professional, and he wanted every one of them to feel the same.

Harmon had a large, outgoing personality. He was as comfortable walking down to the caddie area to share a little encouragement and a few swing tips with the loopers as he was sitting at a large table at Winged Foot, Seminole, or Thunderbird Country Club in Palm Springs, where he worked winters from 1959 on, holding court with the giants of industry and royalty.

Harmon spent the last ten years of his life at Lochinvar Golf Club in Houston. Built in the late 1970s, it was a men-only retreat that featured a Jack Nicklaus–designed course. The opportunity gave Harmon a new lease on life, and it settled him near his son Dick, who had been working at nearby River Oaks since 1977.

Claude Harmon Sr. passed away in Houston while still employed at Lochinvar. One of the great tributes came from his friend Ben Hogan, who wrote: "I know that he would become a Master Professional and he has gone beyond my expectations. Because of his inquisitive attitude toward the golf swing and use of a process of elimination and simplification, he arrived at a point where he could literally put a golf swing together piece by piece, just as a watchmaker would while making a watch. Not only did he put these parts together for himself by winning the Masters tournament, but also for others." In his book *The Pro*, eldest son Butch put his father's place in the realm of golf professionals in very clear perspective: "Unfortunately, my father closed the door on the golden age of golf pros, an age that dated back to Old Tom Morris, who ran a shop in St. Andrews in Scotland and taught the game to the nobility of the day when he wasn't winning championships. What Tom Morris started, Dad finished."

Claude Harmon Sr. and his beloved wife, Alice, had six children, four boys and two girls. For many years, the family had a membership at the Wykagyl County Club in Westchester County, just down the road from Winged Foot. There, Alice and the children could enjoy club life while Harmon worked. The boys all grew up in the game under their father's watchful eye. They practiced and played at Wykagyl until they entered their teens, at which point they began to caddie—and tee it up—at Winged Foot. They carried for notable members like Tommy Armour and Craig Wood and also for the golf celebrity guests that their father brought to the club, like Sam Snead, Jimmy Demaret, Paul Runyan, Ralph Guldahl, and Johnny Revolta, all of whom had won major championships. The boys also hung around and played with many of their father's assistants. In addition, Claude enjoyed watching home movies of golf swings from the greatest players in the game, studying and analyzing their swings and sharing his thoughts on them with his sons. Not surprisingly given those backgrounds, each of the Harmon progeny grew into outstanding players and teachers and found ways to make their livings in golf.

The eldest of those boys was E. Claude "Butch" Harmon Jr., who went to the University of Houston on a four-year golf scholarship. He lasted there only three years, leaving when he became frustrated with his game. A family story relates how he threw a set of clubs he had borrowed from his father into a lake during one of his last frustrating rounds before enlisting in the army, causing his father to remark: "At least you could have joined the navy so you could get my clubs back."

OPPOSITE Claude "Butch" Harmon Jr. began his career as a PGA Professional at Lochinvar Golf Club in Houston. Today he is one of the most in-demand teachers in the game and coaches many of golf's top tour professionals.

Harmon stayed in the army for three years, serving a tour during that time in Vietnam. He earned his PGA Tour card in 1968 and played a total of 21 events through the 1971 season, amassing a meager $8,674 in tournament earnings along the way. Harmon did win the inaugural Broome Country Open (B.C. Open), but it was an unofficial PGA Tour event that year. Looking for another path in the game, he followed in his father's footsteps by moving to Morocco to serve as the personal professional to King Hassan II and also as the teaching professional at the Royal Golf Dar Es Salam complex in Rabat. After returning to the States, Harmon bounced around a bit in various club professional positions. Then, in 1991, the Lochinvar Golf Club in Houston where his father once served hired Butch as its head professional. It was there that he found his calling, as a teacher and coach to the tour's top players. Greg Norman became a pupil and rose from 51st to No. 1 in the world. Then came Tiger Woods, and Harmon started working as his swing doctor in 1993, when Woods was still an amateur, and stayed with him until 2004. Harmon has coached and instructed other top touring professionals, the very best on the game, including Phil Mickelson, Rickie Fowler, Adam Scott, Ernie Els, Dustin Johnson, Brandt Snedeker, and Jimmy Walker. Harmon's success on the lesson tee earned him the top ranking in *Golf Digest*'s top instructor poll for 14 consecutive years, as voted by his peers.

Claude Harmon Sr.'s second son, Craig Harmon, chose to take a road far less traveled than Butch. His first position as an assistant professional came at Lakeside Golf Club in North Hollywood, California, from 1969 through 1971, and he worked summers there and winters at the Thunderbird Country Club, where his father, Claude, had worked for many years. In 1972, his father's former protégé Jack Lumpkin decided to leave his position at Oak Hill Country Club in Rochester, New York. Once Claude heard about that move, he called Lumpkin to ask for his support in getting his then 25-year-old son the position. Lumpkin's first retort was that Craig was too young, but when Harmon reminded his protégé that he helped place Lumpkin at Oak Hill when he was only a few months older, Lumpkin agreed to back Craig's application.

To be sure, Lumpkin's endorsement of Harmon as his successor was important, but what Oak Hill leaders really wanted to know was whether Craig would stay there for some time, or would he want to replace his father at Winged Foot in a few years? The candidate gave them the perfect answer, saying: "I will make Oak Hill my Winged Foot."

Harmon took the reins from Lumpkin in March 1972, and he ended up holding the head professional position at Oak Hill for 42 years, retiring in 2013 and demonstrating all those years that he truly was a man of his word. During that time, Harmon presided over several significant events in the history of the game, among them the PGA Championship in 1980, 2003, and 2013; the Ryder Cup in 1995; the U.S. Amateur in 1998; the U.S. Senior Open in 1984; and the 1989 U.S. Open. He also received his fair share of industry honors, including being named Section Golf Professional of the Year in 1983 and national PGA Golf Professional of the Year 11 years later.

OPPOSITE Prior to the 2013 PGA Championship at Oak Hill Country Club in Rochester, New York, Oak Hill's head professional Craig Harmon, *right*, offered insights to defending champion Rory McIlroy.

In looking back at his career, Craig Harmon could not help but reflect on his roots. "We were lucky to be around an incredible sport," he said. "We grew to appreciate what it did for us and the way Winged Food treated us. To see what a great life it was to be a golf pro."

The third son, Dick Harmon, was a strong player as a teenager, and that led him to San Diego State University, where he quickly became a star on the golf team. He turned professional after college and worked as an assistant for a number of years. Then another of his father's former assistants, Dave Marr, endorsed Dick's application for head professional at River Oaks Country Club in Houston. The year was 1977. Claude Harmon had worked briefly there as head professional during World War II, filling in for Jimmy Demaret, who had been called into the service.

Now, his son was performing the same job. Dick Harmon was 30 years old when he assumed the River Oaks position, and he stayed there for 24 years, earning accolades as a teacher of club members as well as touring professionals like Craig Stadler, Lanny Wadkins, Steve Elkington, Blaine McCallister, and Lucas Glover. "I didn't think there was a better short-game teacher than Dick," Wadkins once told *Golfweek*.

In 2001, Harmon left River Oaks to open the Dick Harmon School of Golf, a learning center with the Houstonian Golf and Country Club. After a couple of years later, he moved his academy to the Redstone Golf Club, which is the host club of the Shell Houston Open. It was not long after he set up shop there that Dick Harmon took ill on a trip to visit his brother Billy in Palm Springs, dying suddenly, just 58 years old.

In many ways William "Billy" Harmon was a golf prodigy. By the time he turned 14, he was shooting in the 60s. At 16, he won the Winged Foot Club Championship, defeating brother Craig in the finals 7 and 6. Along the way, he captured the New York Boys Championship and the Met Junior Championship. Deemed the most naturally talented golfer of the four brothers, Billy followed Dick to San Diego State University to play college golf on a full-ride scholarship. He proved to be an instant success, but by the end of his freshman year he had lost his game, and also his focus in life, as he began to struggle with addictions to drugs and alcohol. He left school after just one year and enlisted in the marines.

Following his term of service, Billy Harmon returned to golf, holding several positions as golf professional before beginning what became a very successful stint as a tour caddie. Harmon hooked up with Jay Haas, a young player who appeared destined to become a solid competitor, and they worked together for roughly a decade. Then, in 1987, Billy left the nomadic life of a tour caddie for more stable surroundings, going to work for his brother Craig at Oak Hill as the club got ready for the 1989 U.S. Open. Once that championship was done, Harmon took the head professional position at the tony Newport Golf Club, in Newport, Rhode Island. While there, the club hosted the 1995 U.S. Amateur, which was one way of celebrating the centennial of its hosting the inaugural event. Tiger Woods won the 1995 edition, beating future Walker Cup Captain Buddy Marucci in the finals.

Today, Billy Harmon serves as director of instruction at the Toscana Country Club in Indian Wells, California. Now clean and sober after struggling with his addictions for many years, he has found happiness in his life and his work. In 2010, Harmon and his wife, Robin, created the Harmon Recovery Foundation, which provides alcohol and drug treatment programs. In addition to his teaching at Toscana, he has appeared on the Golf Channel in a variety of capacities and is consistently recognized by leading golf publications as a top 100 instructor.

It seems only right that there should still be a Claude Harmon in golf, and there is, in Claude Harmon III. The grandson of Claude Sr. and son of Butch, he grew up on the lesson tee, and as a young man he often shot video of the touring professionals his father Butch was teaching. After graduating from Stephen F. Austin State University in Texas, he went to work for his father at the Lochinvar in Houston, and it wasn't long before he was working with club members on their games.

While Claude Harmon III enjoyed his time in Houston, he also found ways to ply his trade and expand his knowledge of the golf swing outside of the United States. He worked in Scotland, Portugal, Dubai, and Macau and competed full-time on the European Tour from 2002 to 2006. During his career, he has coached the likes of Ernie Els, Brooks Koepka, Yani Tseng, Trevor Immelman, Adam Scott, Graeme McDowell, Gary Woodland, Peter Uihlein, and Darren Clarke. Currently, he serves as the director of instruction at the Butch Harmon Floridian, an exclusive club in the Sunshine State, oftentimes working alongside his dad.

No discussion of top PGA of America Professionals during this period would be complete without mentioning Manuel de la Torre. As recipient of the inaugural PGA Teacher of the Year Award, in 1986, he was the first Association member to be honored by his peers as its premier instructor. In later years, the longstanding head professional at the Milwaukee Country Club also gained berths in the World Golf Teachers Hall of Fame and the PGA of America Hall of Fame. He was especially well-known for his teaching skills, and his long list of students not only included hundreds of club members but also several top touring professionals, among them World Golf Hall of Famer Carol Mann, Masters winner Tommy Aaron, U.S. Women's Open champion Martha Nause, and Women's British Open titleholder Sherri Steinhauer.

The son of a Spanish golf professional, de la Torre was born in 1921 in his parents' apartment above the golf shop at the Real Club de la Puerta de Hierro in Madrid, where his father, Angel, who was a five-time national champion in Spain, served as the head golf professional. De la Torre the Elder emigrated to the States a year after Manuel's birth to work as a golf professional, first at the Timber Point Golf Course in Great River on Long Island and later at the newly opened Pasatiempo Golf Club in Northern California, where the great golf course architect Alister MacKenzie and the notable amateur player Marion Hollins were residing. The Spaniard enjoyed life in America, but the economic hardships of the Great Depression were making it more and more difficult for golf professionals to prosper in the United States, so he returned with his family to his native land, in 1932.

Civil War broke out in Spain in 1936, while Angel de la Torre was in the United States on business. He feared for his safety if he went back to Spain, so he stayed in America and waited five months for his wife and two sons, Manuel and Luis, to complete a harrowing journey to America. Safely in the United States, Manuel de la Torre was able to earn a scholarship to study at Northwestern University and also to play on the golf team. He was good enough to make it to the finals of the NCAAs in 1942, losing to Frank "Sandy" Tatum of Stanford, who would go on to become president of the USGA.

De la Torre fought for the U.S. Army in Europe for a year during World War II, serving on or near the frontlines and returning to the States only after the Germans surrendered. Once he was back in America, de la Torre took a job as an assistant professional at the Lake Shore Country Club in Chicago, where his father held forth as the head professional. Then, in 1951, Manuel became the head professional at the Milwaukee Country Club. It was a position he would hold until 1996.

De la Torre joined the PGA and in 1955 started a three-year stint as president of the Wisconsin PGA Section. Over time, that group bestowed a number of honors upon de la Torre, presenting him with its Horton Smith Award three times and thrice naming him Teacher of the Year.

As a golf instructor, de la Torre became a strong proponent of the approach of English Professional Ernest Jones, a dear friend of his father's who had lost his right leg while fighting in World War I. "The Ernest Jones view is a holistic view of the movement, and it coincides with the physics of motion, velocity, and force," de la Torre wrote in his book, *Understanding the Golf Swing*. "A great difference is that the Jones concept deals with the movement of the club in concert with these basic principles and not with the movement of the body and its position so important in the teachings of others."

Manuel de la Torre also was a premier player as a PGA Professional. Among his victories were five Wisconsin State Opens, five Wisconsin PGA Championships, the 1973 National Open Seniors Classic, and the 1987 Wisconsin PGA Senior Championship.

CHAPTER

SIX

Through the 1990s

olf continued to grow and change in very big ways as the PGA of America entered its fourth decade, and so did the Association, marking its 60th birthday in 1976 as the United States celebrated its bicentennial. Television coverage of the royal and ancient game continued to expand and improve, and the introduction of cable service as a complement to over-air broadcasts opened an inconceivable number of channels and the age of media specialization.

Golf as programming was more available than ever before, and that spurred interest in the sport from spectating and participatory standpoints. At the same time, the commerce of course operations expanded through the introduction of multicourse management companies and the success of relatively new businesses such as the ClubCorp, which bought and managed clubs and resorts like Inverrary, Firestone, and Pinehurst; and Landmark, which developed a number of top courses and destinations, Kiawah Island and PGA West among them. That boosted the course and club inventory for players and further elevated golf's profile. So, too, did a rash of construction of new courses, instigated in many ways by a mandate that came out of a National Golf Foundation report to "build a course a day" over the next several years to satisfy what it believed was going to be a massive rise in demand for new places to play.

That era also saw the emergence of modern golf course architects like Pete Dye, who happily pushed the design envelope in heretofore unimagined ways in places like Oak Tree in Oklahoma and Harbour Town on Hilton Head Island. During this period, Dye also laid out the celebrated Stadium Course at TPC Sawgrass, the dramatic angles and maddening undulations of which both enraged the touring professionals who had to play the track and ushered in the era of the Tournament Players Club.

The Ryder Cup received a big boost in 1979 when it was determined that golfers from the Continent could combine with the Brits and Irish to form one European team. Competition increased dramatically, and so did the level of play, and the matches soon became one of the most popular events in professional sports. Recreational players enjoyed a boon as well, thanks to remarkable advances in the

PREVIOUS PAGE Bob Ford became the model for the modern era PGA Professional by excelling at the business of golf, being a top-ranked teacher, mentoring assistant professionals, and accomplishing numerous competitive achievements. OPPOSITE The PGA Championship was first televised in 1958, the year that the format changed from match play to stroke play.

development of new golf clubs and balls, and they clamored to get a hold of the latest and greatest pieces of equipment, such as the perimeter-weighted Eye 2 irons from Ping; the first metal woods, by Gary Adams of TaylorMade; the oversized and eminently playable Big Bertha drivers from Callaway; and at the turn of the 21st century the solid-core, urethane-covered Pro V1 golf ball from Titleist. It was an exciting time in that part of the business, and nowhere was that development more evident that at the annual PGA Merchandise Show, which had grown from a quaint annual gathering of club professionals and equipment and apparel makers to a huge enterprise bringing together thousands of exhibitors and PGA Professionals at the Orange County Convention Center in Orlando, Florida, each January.

The beginning of this period also saw the final barrier to PGA membership broken down, as a 1978 class action lawsuit brought against the Association compelled the PGA to allow women to become members. This cleared the way for a young assistant professional in Atlanta named Barrie Naismith to become the first female Class A Professional. More than two decades later, the glass ceiling in the PGA of America administration was cracked when Sue Fiscoe was elected secretary of the Northern California Section. Then, in 2005, she was named its president, becoming in the process the first woman to serve as the leader of a Section in the history of the organization.

To be sure, all was not wine and roses during this era, and there were problems in the form of serious economic recessions, the Islamic

From its humble beginnings in 1954, the PGA Merchandise Show in Orlando has grown into an annual gathering of more than 40,000 golf industry professionals from nearly 75 countries around the globe.

revolution in Iran and the hostage crisis that accompanied it, and the Soviet invasion of Afghanistan. But the United States entered a new period of prosperity in the early 1980s, and the years through the end of the 20th century came to be regarded as among the some of the calmest and most productive in America's history, with steady economic growth and the conclusion of the Cold War that was most dramatically signified with the tearing down of the Berlin Wall in 1989.

Golf, and the PGA, found ways to weather the tough times in fine fettle and to do well once things turned around. The Association kept on promoting, and producing, a very high level of PGA Professionals who adapted to the ways the game was changing and worked hard to serve their constituency even better than before.

Bob Nye emerged as a PGA Professional of note during this period, as did several members of his family. A physical education teacher from Springfield, Massachusetts, Nye who grew to become one of the most acclaimed coaches in NCAA golf history when he took over an all but nonexistent program at the College of Wooster in Ohio and grew it into one of the finest Division III operations in the land. Along the way, he mentored 14 future PGA Professionals. Three of those happened to be his sons, Greg, Scott, and Gary, and they all make their livings in the game today.

Bob Nye's parents were both employed at the local telephone company in Springfield, Massachusetts, with his father working on the lines in the field while his mother labored as a switchboard operator. Nye was a talented athlete as a boy, and one of the games he fancied was golf. He had access to a number of municipal courses but was lucky to be singled out and mentored by Connecticut PGA Section legend John Raimondi at the Veterans Memorial Golf Course.

Nye shares that he did "a little caddying and a lot of playing" at Memorial during his high

school years, and when he was 16, he began to work for Raimondi at the course. When it came time for college, Nye decided to stay local and attend Springfield College, a private school that was recognized for excellence in the field of physical education. He enjoyed his first years there because, in his words, it combined a curriculum of a teacher's college with "all the sciences for the physical education portion of it. I really got into the kinesiology and physiology of exercise and the testing of athletes for flight angles of balls, a javelin being thrown, or shot being put. Those kinds of things just intrigued the heck out of me."

The already three-year-long Korean War interrupted Nye's college education when he was drafted into the army in 1953. He was routed directly into the infantry, and his unit was destined for combat at the completion of their 16-week basic training. Luckily for Nye, the Asian conflict ended just four weeks before that program ended. As a result, he was able to spend the remainder of his army career in the United States before returning to Springfield College to complete his undergraduate studies.

In the fall of 1958, Nye began his teaching career, as a physical education teacher in a New Jersey high school. Six years later, he moved to the College of Wooster, which was located in the small Ohio town of the same name. Initially, he was to coach the soccer team, but five years into his work there, school administrators asked Nye to take over its golf operations as well.

The college owned a 9-hole golf course that had been built during the Great Depression with funds from a New Deal agency. For years, the layout had been run on a shoestring and as a free amenity for all students, faculty, and their families, its only revenues coming from green fees. Nye sought to change that first by creating a makeshift pro shop in a shack on the property that offered golf balls, gloves, and an extremely limited soft goods inventory. Then he built up a fleet of golf carts and added a small practice facility.

As he was doing all he could to squeeze some money out of the golf course for his employer, Nye attended his first PGA education seminar on merchandising and golf shop operations. A questionnaire was passed around for participants to fill out, and one of the queries wondered about the type of lighting they used in their golf shops. Nye was truthful when he wrote: "One 100-watt bulb." In reviewing the questionnaires before the session formally began, the presenter suddenly stopped, stared at the paper in his hand, and asked, "Who in the heck wrote 'a 100-watt bulb'?" Nye raised his hand and explained that that one bulb hanging from the center of the ceiling lighted his total shop. To that, the presented replied, "I am not sure this seminar will be much help to your operation." Truth be told, it was, and Nye was quick to recognize the value of the PGA educational and training programs. In fact, he soon entered the PGA Apprentice Program as a nonmember head professional, which ultimately earned him Class A membership in 1974. Nye proudly recalls being in one of the first PGA Business Schools. To attend, he traveled to Hartford, Connecticut, where Bill Strausbaugh made a lasting impression on the college coach and educator.

Nye had taken over the men's golf team three years into his tenure at Wooster after being asked to trade his spring duties as an assistant with the track squad. Two of his first steps were to establish a combination preseason physical assessment and training program and schedule the school's first-ever spring break golf team trip. His new team met his first move with a touch of bewilderment, while the second was greeted with great enthusiasm.

One of his early charges at Wooster was Tom Wilcox, who would go on to become a PGA Master Professional and hold head professional positions at a number of top American clubs, among them Sankaty Head on Nantucket; the Philadelphia Country Club; the Governors Club in Chapel Hill, North Carolina; and the Quintero Golf Club and Blackstone Country Club outside Phoenix. Another player of note was Gary Welshhans, who earned All-American honors each of his four years at Wooster and then went on to become the head golf professional at the Wooster Country Club, where he has worked the past 39 years.

It wasn't long before Nye's three sons were coming through the program as well. In 1975, Greg helped lead the team to the first-ever NCAA Division III Championship as a freshman and earned second team All-America honors. In his three subsequent seasons, he was named a First-Team All-American largely on the strength of second-, fourth-, and sixth-place finishes in the national championship. Greg was also the individual champion in the

ABOVE Northern California PGA Professional Sue Fiscoe became the first woman elected a Section President and a PGA District Director.

Valhalla Golf Club, a PGA of America property, has hosted three PGA Championships,
two Senior PGA Championships, a Ryder Cup, and a PGA Professional Championship.

Ohio Athletic Conference in his final two years at Wooster.

Following college, and his father, Greg made his way into the coaching ranks, first as an assistant at Duke University and then as head coach at Bowling Green State University. Eight years later, he took the head job at Penn State University, where he continues to lead the golf team.

Second son Scott also opted to attend the College of Wooster. After earning All-American honors all four years there, he became a PGA Professional, taking his first head job in 1990 at the Country Club of York in Pennsylvania just north of the Maryland state line. During his tenure there, he served as host professional for the 1999 U.S. Junior Amateur. Then, in 2000, he moved to the Merion Golf Club, where he has twice been honored with the Philadelphia PGA Section Horton Smith Award while establishing a strong reputation for developing outstanding assistant professionals. In 2005, he served as host professional for the U.S. Amateur, and eight years after that, his club was the site of the U.S. Open.

Youngest son Gary played for Bob Nye at the College of Wooster from 1992 through 1996, graduating the year of his father's retirement, and his first position in the golf business post-Wooster was a four-year stint at Burning Tree Club in Bethesda, Maryland. That was followed by a tandem of seasonal positions working for Bob Ford at Oakmont and Seminole for a total of two years. Following two years at Old Memorial Golf Club in the Tampa area, Gary Nye obtained his first head professional position at the prestigious Rolling Rock Club near Ligonier, Pennsylvania, for eight years. Today, he is the director of golf at the prominent Stock Farm Club in the Big Sky Country of Montana.

During a recent College of Wooster golf reunion, the group was able to count 14 past team members who went on to become PGA Professionals after playing for Coach Nye. Over his 30 years there, Bob Nye took his Wooster golf team to 23 NCAA National Championships.

After retiring from the College of Wooster, Nye wondered for a while what he would do next. The answer came when one of his former players, Tom Wilcox, asked him if he wanted to teach part-time at the Wooster Country Club. Nye jumped at the opportunity, and he works there to this day.

Pete Davison was one of those golfers who determined during his college playing days that he would one day make a living in the game, and that is exactly what he began to do after playing for three years on the University of Georgia team. He thought at first that he would become a traditional golf professional, having worked summers during school at the Standard Club in Atlanta and the Augusta Country Club in his hometown of Augusta, Georgia. And that appeared to be the direction he was taking when he secured an assistant's position after college with the renowned teaching professional Davis Love Jr. at the Atlanta Country Club, but fate intervened several years later, in the form of an offer to be the first professional at the first TPC club at Sawgrass and later as the person in charge of the entire TPC operation, and that led Davison down an entirely different career path.

After working with Love in Atlanta, Davison moved to Upstate New York to take an assistant's position at the prestigious Oak Hill Country Club with a good friend of his former boss's, Jack Lumpkin. Like Love, Lumpkin was a highly regarded professional who enjoyed mentoring young assistants. Among other things, he encouraged Davison to compete in tournaments,

OPPOSITE Jack Lumpkin, the 1995 PGA of America Teacher of the Year, has left an indelible mark in guiding both the premier and amateur player.

and the young Georgian responded with several strong tournament performances, qualifying for the 1971 U.S. Open at Merion and making it all the way to the final qualifying round for Q-School. He missed getting his PGA Tour card by 1 stroke.

The following winter, Davison secured a winter teaching gig at the Dorado Beach Hotel, which at the time was considered one of the top resort destinations in the world, and then a summer position on Long Island under Joe Moresco at the Woodmere Club. For the next two years, Davison worked both those jobs. He also continued to tee it up in tournaments, and it was in the fall of 1973 that he captured the Metropolitan Open, which was at one time considered a professional major and had evolved into one of the strongest regional tourneys in the country. With the backing of several Woodmere members, Davison attempted to make a living on the PGA Tour the following season. "I had some decent moments, but not enough of them," he says. "It became evident that unless

something drastic happened, I wasn't going to be able to keep my card. At the time, I had a wife, two children and a dog to worry about, so I had to consider other opportunities."

The best opportunity came in the form of a job with the Golf Club at Middle Bay on Long Island, and he served there for five years. Then, as he was beginning his sixth season at Middle Bay, he received a letter from the PGA of America with a job notice for the head professional position at a new golf club that was opening in Ponte Vedra Beach, Florida. The missive had been sent to every PGA member throughout the United States to initiate a search for a professional who would head up the golf operation at the PGA Tour's Tournament Players Club (TPC), which would feature a Pete Dye-designed golf course and serve as the permanent home to the tournament now known as The Players Championship.

Davison was impressed by the job description and wrote a cover letter that summarized his interest in the position and his qualifications.

ABOVE One of the most decorated PGA of America members, Ken Morton Sr., is regarded as one of the most innovative and guiding forces in player development. OPPOSITE Two of sport's all-time heavyweights, Jack Nicklaus and Muhammad Ali, connected at Valhalla Golf Club prior to the 1996 PGA Championship. Nicklaus designed the course in Ali's hometown of Louisville, Kentucky.

Much to his surprise, the search committee chose him as one of five final candidates to be interviewed by PGA Tour Commissioner Deane Beman, and then Beman offered Davison the job.

From the beginning Commissioner Beman related to Davison that he would be responsible for executing all golf operations, adding: "I don't know what to tell you to do, but everything has to be first-class." Beman had staked his future as commissioner on the concept of the PGA Tour and its players owning their own course to host their tournament. Now, he was entrusting his chosen golf professional to deliver a product that would validate his vision.

It had been a major battle for Beman to earn board and player approval for the TPC at Sawgrass, and many viewed the move as risky and well outside the focus of their business model, however Beman believed it was not only the right move for the players, but also a necessary shift needed to elevate the image of the players and their tour.

The commissioner was farsighted in his expectation for the club's operation to be superior, and his choice to lead that charge was equal to the challenge. Davison drew on his experiences from his career as an assistant and head professional to establish a system that would deliver the five-star service the commissioner demanded. For example, Davison remembered how Love had always carried around a yellow legal pad at Atlanta, filling its pages through the days and often at nights with notes about the golf swing as well as his business operations. So, Davison adopted his mentor's habit, using the yellow legal pad as his daily road map and maintaining one hard and firm rule: He never left the office at the end of the day unless everything he had deemed necessary on his pad was completed and crossed out.

Delayed by a year due to grow-in conditions, the first Players Championship to be contested over the players' own course took place in March 1982. The national broadcast of the event brought instant attention and notoriety to the difficult Pete Dye design. While many of the players were harsh with their criticism of the course, largely due to its rough virgin surrounds that encased only 45 acres of maintained turf, Beman's concept for stadium golf was an instant hit with spectators and the television audience.

The first Players Championship made a big splash in more than one way. The lasting impression of champion Jerry Pate tossing both Pete Dye and Commissioner Beman off the railroad tie-supported 18th green into the bordering lake served as an exclamation point to the tournament and concept. Soon after, golf community developers were calling the PGA Tour to see how they could build a TPC in their community. The notion was novel, as Beman had not originally considered building more than one course for his organization.

After considering the opportunity, two contracts were quickly signed for facilities in Coral Springs, Florida, near Fort Lauderdale (now TPC Eagle Trace) and Castle Rock, Colorado, outside Denver (the former TPC Plum Creek). When the Tour decided to venture into the multicourse market, it promoted Davison to general manager and director of golf at TPC Sawgrass, then tasked him with the responsibility of creating the framework that would assure that the quality and success from that first operation could be exported to other facilities that would bear the PGA Tour and TPC brand.

To do so, Davison began with his carefully prepared TPC Sawgrass operating procedures and then expanded them into extensive, step-by-step operating manuals, also studying high-end hotel chains to learn how to create consistency and continuity in operations from location to location. No doubt, he used a yellow legal pad to write down his thoughts and ideas.

Following 25 years of service to the PGA Tour, Davison retired at the end of 2004.

He left behind a legacy that earned him and PGA Tour's network of clubs nearly every imaginable award in the golf industry and solidified the model that PGA Professionals are fully capable of leading club operations at a level equal to or exceeding professionals drawn from other management disciplines.

For Ken Morton Sr., his entrée to golf lead right to the caddie yard, and he viewed it in the beginning simply as a way to make money as a young boy growing up in Sacramento, California. It turned out to be an introduction to a game that would become his life. From that first loop, he fell hard for the sport. Morton loved the atmosphere around the Del Paso Country Club and offered to help out wherever he could. In addition to carrying bags for members, Morton handpicked the practice facility, cleaned members' clubs, and worked in the golf shop. The head professional at Del Paso, Frank Mintz Sr., took a special interest in the hardworking caddie, and that eventually turned into free golf lessons, which Morton began taking when was about 14 years old.

He was a natural talent, and in his senior year at El Camino Fundamental High School, he led his golf team to the Northern California State Championship, where he also captured the individual state championship. That same year, Morton took a job at the Haggin Oaks facility in town as a part-time starter, beginning a relationship with the head professional, Tom LoPresti, which soon led to Morton becoming his teaching assistant.

Faithfully committed to LoPresti for the next dozens years or so, Morton continued to grow and prosper in his role there. Then, LoPresti approached him with an offer. "I am going to need someone to replace me someday," the old pro said to Morton. "How would you like to be my partner?" LoPresti was a legend in Sacramento at the time, a 63-year-old who had spent 40 years at Haggin Oaks. He had just offered Morton the job of co-head professional. Morton accepted, and the two worked together for another 23 years.

Not long after assuming that position, Morton became a member of the faculty of an upcoming PGA Business School scheduled for Sacramento. That led to a regular commitment to participate in those schools on a regular basis and to apply what he learned from them in his work.

Morton continues to play a major role in PGA Education 35 years later, and he also benefits from all it has to offer. In addition, he has served as a subject matter expert working with the PGA to build new programs over the decades that included the Golf Professional Training Program, the PGA Certified Professional Program, the new Master Professional Program, and Professional Golf Management Program. "I could have never, ever been anywhere near the professional I turned out to be without those experiences," he says. "There is no way I ever could have created or bought that education outside of the PGA."

Recalling his caddie years, Morton likes to reminisce on how that early work experience changed his life. "All of us kids who started out with Frank Mintz Sr. and Tommy LoPresti, we were really from the other side of the tracks and had the opportunity to either go to the bad way or the good way of life," he says. "To have someone there to support us and to say, 'You know, Ken, the way you treated that member really wasn't nice. If you want to stay in the golf business, you should talk to them like this.' You realized as a caddie that the better service you give, the better tips that you get, and the more jobs that you got, and the more requests that you got. You learned about customer service at a very early age." Continuing his thought process, Morton looks at the broad collection of golf professionals who came into the game from

the 1940s to the 1960s, and then offered this rhetorical question: "Who knows where they would have turned out had it not been for golf?"

In 1983 he created the Sacramento Area Youth Golf Association program SAY Golf. "With golf courses relying more on carts there was this tremendous change taking place. When I was growing up, kids like me didn't have a lot of opportunities available to us in society—but we did thorough golf. All that was disappearing, so we worked to create an organized program to bring young people into the game.

SAY Golf introduced tens of thousands of young boys and girls to golf and in 1999 became an official chapter of the First Tee. Later, Morton created another initiative called Saving Strokes, which was designed to deal with the mental and physical needs of stroke victims. Founded in Sacramento, it now operates in 16 unique sites in California, Arizona, Utah, and Nevada and serves more than 1,000 participants. It also stands as yet one more testament to Ken Morton's love of golf and his desire to give the game as much as it has given him.

Sandy Lumpkin LaBauve came into the world the second child to a serious golfing family. Her father is Jack Lumpkin, the noted PGA member who worked as an assistant to Claude Harmon at Winged Foot, Seminole, and Thunderbird; served as head professional at Oak Hill and Cherokee; taught at Pinehurst and still gives lessons at the Sea Island resort in southeast Georgia as its senior director of instruction. Sherry, her mother, helped her husband Jack design, decorate, and stock his golf shops and also assisted with some of his junior programs. Her brother Jay became a recognized instructor and also a player of some repute, winning the 1987 PGA Professional National Championship. Is it any wonder given those bloodlines that Sandy, too, gravitated to the game?

Sandy was a strong player as a teenager, carrying a 3 handicap and being good enough to earn a golf scholarship to the University of Georgia, where her father had competed. She lettered at Georgia for three years before leaving college to follow her heart. A fellow teammate had introduced her to a young assistant professional named Mike LaBauve on a blind date. A graduate of Louisiana State University and a former member of the golf team there, he was trying to make it as a touring professional while working outside operations at Palmetto Dunes on Hilton Head Island. College may have been the more sensible choice for Sandy, but she was in love and wanted to get married, so Lumpkin dropped out of Georgia to join LaBauve at Palmetto Dunes.

Later, she realized that leaving school was a mistake and enrolled at Georgia Southern, in part because it was close to Hilton Head, where LaBauve continued to work. Shortly after receiving her degree, Sandy's father, Jack, took a job at the Pinehurst resort. One of his first moves was to ask LaBauve to be his first assistant, and the family was reunited in the Carolina Sandhills, with Sandy and Mike marrying there in the summer of 1981.

At Pinehurst Mike's teaching was extensive, working with club members and resort guests and as a support instructor under Lumpkin during Golf Digest School sessions when they were held at the resort. During this period, Sandy worked in the hotel's sales and marketing department. She was not entirely happy with her job and one day after work asked her husband, "What do you think about me turning pro?" His first reaction was a wry one, wondering if there already weren't too many golf professionals in the family, but he was actually quite supportive of the idea.

Late in 1983, the young couple left Pinehurst for the winter season to go to Florida. Sandy was seeking an entry-level assistant position in order to take care of the six-month work requirement for her application as a PGA apprentice. At the same time, Mike wanted to test his competitive game on the Florida mini-tour circuits. Sandy landed a position at Inverrary Country Club and soon after accrued the necessary credits needed to apply to the PGA Apprentice program.

As their winter venture ended, the couple eventually headed to the Phoenix, Arizona, area. Along the way, Sandy made an attempt at qualifying for the LPGA Tour at Sweetwater Country Club in Sugar Land, Texas, where she missed earning her card by 2 strokes. A little disillusioned, she decided to take a break from golf, but Sandy soon realized she missed the game and went back to work in it, as an assistant at Scottsdale's Gainey Ranch Golf Club. It was during her interview with director of golf Dan Desmond that she shared that her main career interest was to obtain membership in the LPGA Teaching Division, since she felt that instruction was going to be her eventual path. "He looked me straight in the eyes and said, 'You can work here only if you apply to both," she recalled. "He then said, 'I want you to do that because this is what you see yourself doing at this point, but you have so much life ahead of you and you have no idea of where you are going to go, so you need to broaden your base and learn as much as you can about the entire business.'" LaBauve agreed, realizing that the education programs of the two leading professional associations actually complimented each other. At the time, the LPGA was heavily weighted in a teaching curriculum while the PGA offered a more extensive education program that would expose her to all facets of the game.

OPPOSITE Sandy LaBauve, the daughter of famed instructor Jack Lumpkin, is one of the top PGA Teaching Professionals in the country and founded the LPGA Junior Girls Golf Club.

In 1989 Kerry Graham, national president of the LPGA Teaching Division, approached LaBauve with a problem that the LPGA was facing locally, saying: "We have a dilemma in Arizona right now in the sense that a lot of girls come out in the beginning and want to learn to play the game, but no girls are playing tournament golf here. For some reason, there is a huge loss of interest in golf after they get introduced to the game. I think that the answer is the Girl Scouts. It's a big organization of girls that already exists, and if we could do some clinics for them, then possibly we'll have a whole group of girls we can turn into golfers."

LaBauve, who was pregnant at the time and still an assistant at Gainey Ranch, jumped on the idea. In the beginning, clinics were taught over a six-week period, and Girl Scouts were bused in from all over the state. The program initially appeared to be a success, but it presented the organizers with something of a problem, for they now had hundreds of novice graduates and no follow-up program to which they could advance and develop even deeper ties to the game. That prompted LaBauve to create a series of tournaments where the competition was often in partner formats so the fear of failure or an opportunity of embarrassment was minimized. Originally, she called this initiative the Junior Girls Golf Club of Arizona, and it quickly grew to be a regional success. The next step was to take it national, as Girls Golf, and it has since grown to include more than over 250 local clubs throughout the United States. More than 30,000 girls participate, upwards of 150,000 girls have been introduced to golf through the program, all told, and there are now international outreach offerings in Canada, New Zealand, and Australia.

For her role in creating and then continuing with Girls Golf, LaBauve has received numerous honors. Among her most prized is the 2008 LPGA For the Love of the Game Award that was presented at that year's Kraft Nabisco Championship Gala at Mission Hills Country Club. One year later, in conjunction with the 20th anniversary of the founding of Girls Golf, the organization established the Sherry G. Lumpkin Founders Award, in honor of LaBauve's mother and to "recognize an individual who demonstrates incredible passion, ongoing commitment, and extraordinary dedication to securing the game's future by cultivating interest among girls in the game of golf."

Shortly after founding the Girls Golf program in 1989, LaBauve left her position at Gainey Ranch to join her husband, Mike, at the Stonecreek Golf Club. There, they built an outstanding instruction program during a six-year tenure at that facility. While at Stonecreek, Mike was named the Southwest Section Player of the Year in 1989 and the Section Teacher of the Year in 1987 and 1993. He also became one of *Golf Magazine*'s Top 100 Instructors as well as the full-time head instructor for Golf Digest Schools. As for Sandy, she continued her strong support of the Girls Golf program as a consultant, frequently traveling to assist in the expansion of the program. She also gained recognition as a Top 100 Teacher in the World from *Golf Magazine* and obtained her PGA Class A membership.

In 1995, the couple took their LaBauve Golf program across town to the new Westin Kierland Resort and Spa in Scottsdale. They have been there ever since. Their expanded programs continued to earn national and worldwide acclaim. Mike won his third Southwest Section PGA Teacher of the Year honor in 2001, and Sandy became an instructor

OPPOSITE Brian Gaffney, the PGA Head Professional at Quaker Ridge Golf Club in Scarsdale, New York, won a playoff in the PGA Professional Championship to earn a PGA Championship berth in 2015 at Whistling Straits. He then earned nationwide attention by making the 36-hole cut in a field that featured 96 of the top 100 players in the world.

with Golf Digest Schools in 1998. She was voted the 1998 Southwest Section PGA Teacher of the Year and in 2010 was inducted into the Arizona Golf Hall of Fame.

In addition to their work in golf, the couple has raised two talented daughters, one of whom, Lindy, is making the game a career. After lettering for four years on the women's golf team at LSU, her father's alma mater, and earning a degree in economics, she became the women's golf coach at the University of South Carolina Beaufort. Following two successful seasons, she opted to leave team coaching for an apprentice professional position at the Lodge at Sea Island where she will be under her grandfather's watchful eye as she strives to expand her instruction knowledge with emphasis in short game improvement.

Some years ago, the PGA of America produced an advertisement that extolled the virtues of its club professionals and detailed the many things they have to do, and do well, in order to prosper in their business, like merchandising golf apparel and mentoring aspiring assistants, teaching lessons and running tournaments, handling rules disputes and dealing with club politics. Another item on the list was playing golf—with their members, to be sure, but also in competitions on local and national levels. That made good sense because PGA Professionals are first and foremost golfers, and the vast majority of them developed their initial passion for the game as players.

It was a powerful bit of promotion that spoke to the many talents PGA members possess, but it inadvertently highlighted an increasingly difficult part of that job: maintaining a high level of skill as a player. The job of club professional now entails so many different aspects and demands that it is difficult for many to find the time to practice and play. There simply are not enough hours in the day anymore to nurture a game that truly holds up in competition.

Then, there is the cold truth that teeing it in tournaments can sometimes be a detriment to the employment security of a club professional, as some facilities prefer that their professionals be around their shops and practice ranges to service their customers and members, not trying to go low in tournaments.

With those matters in mind, it is hard not to admire the PGA club professional who plays, and plays well, as he or she handles all the other duties the position entails. In fact, that talent is something worth celebrating, and perhaps no one in the modern era has demonstrated more deftness in that area than Bob Ford.

Ford holds down two of the biggest jobs in golf as the head professional at the Oakmont Country Club outside Pittsburgh, Pennsylvania, in the summer season and at the esteemed Seminole Golf Club in Juno Beach, Florida, in the winter. What makes Ford's record as a head golf professional even more notable is that he has managed to distinguish himself as a player at the same time.

For example, he has qualified and played in 10 PGA Championships, the first in 1981 and the last in 2005. Ford has also competed in three U.S. Opens, making the cut in two of them. In addition, the man who began his golf career as a young caddie has played in five Senior PGA Championships and two U.S. Senior Opens. The very strong Tri-State PGA Section has named Ford its Player of the Year 10 times, and in 1988 he accepted the award for being the PGA's Professional Player of the Year, 12 months after the association had honored him as its PGA Golf Professional of the Year. Pretty heady stuff, to be sure, and no one was really surprised that in 2005 Ford was inducted into the PGA Hall of Fame.

When one looks back on such a storied playing career and Ford's ability to wear so many hats so well, one moment stands out from all the others. That would be the time in 1983 when the then-

29-year-old qualified for the U.S. Open being held at Oakmont. He not only made the cut of that year's national championship and finished tied for 26th as he played before a hometown crowd, but also managed to run the tournament's merchandising operation at the same time. In those days, the host club professional oversaw that business and took all the financial risk, which meant that Ford carried a very different mental burden than his fellow competitors as he walked the course during the day. Instead of pounding balls on the range after his rounds, he retreated to his office to crunch numbers on his calculator.

Ford has not played in an Open for a while, but that does not mean he has given up competing. "I don't play tournaments as much as I once did, but I still have that desire to win, and I still believe I am going to win whatever I enter an event," he says. "I also realize that I am not as good as I once was, even though I feel just as good, and I understand that when it comes to national tournaments, it's just not a fair fight."

It was the prospect of playing professionally and being that individual who made his living teeing it in tournaments that drove Ford as a young golfer. Born in Pittsburgh and raised in Philadelphia, he went to work as an assistant for then Oakmont head professional Lew Worsham after graduating from the University of Tampa in 1975 because he thought his new boss could help him accomplish that goal. After all, the Chin, as Worsham was affectionately called, knew what it took, having won six times in his playing career on the PGA Tour, including the 1947 U.S. Open.

Ford spent five summers as an assistant at Oakmont, and when he wasn't giving lessons or selling golf shirts he was tending to a vegetable garden Worsham had established at the back of the practice range. With his boss's encouragement, Ford also teed it up regularly, wining the Tri-State Open his first year there

but failing in his four attempts as an Oakmont assistant to make it through Q-School. He was dismayed, to be sure, but then the club leaders at Oakmont asked Ford to take over as their head professional after Worsham retired. Ford assumed the top position in 1980 when he was only 25 years old.

Though he gave up his vision of competing regularly on the PGA Tour, Ford did not lose his passion for playing, and he entered dozens of sectional tournaments over the next several decades. He was good enough to have won a bunch of those and to have qualified for 21 professional majors, but the strongest measuring stick of his talents as a PGA club professional on and off the course is that Ford played his way into nine of those majors while excelling at not one but two of the biggest jobs in golf.

Of course, competing is just one of many things Ford does exceptionally well. He is also known as a superb merchandiser, and his pro shops have the feel of a high-end retail store. He is also a mentor of the highest order and prides himself on the way he has trained dozens of young professionals over the years and prepared them for the head professional positions he holds today. Ford is the consummate host and runs his golf operations with a warm and efficient manner that makes everyone, members and guests alike, feel welcome.

Some form of retirement is looming for Ford. He says he plans to leave Oakmont after it hosts the 2016 U.S. Open, but he has no plans to stop competing. "I'm already thinking about going over to play in the British Senior. I have not played in one of those since 2004, and I know my chances are not very good—but you never know."

Still a competitor after all these years, and a very strong one at that. His record and desire speak for themselves.

CHAPTER

SEVEN

Modern PGA Professionals

olf was looking stronger and healthier at the start of this era than at any other time in its history. Developers had taken the National Golf Foundation's "course-a-day" edict to heart and were building new layouts all over the United States. That provided a lot of new places for people to play and also ensured there were ample job openings for golf professionals and those who sought employment in other parts of that business.

The advances in golf equipment and the products that were introduced as a result of them, like the Pro V1 ball and the Great Big Bertha driver, both electrified a playing public that wanted nothing more than to shave a few shots off their games and also helped grow sales for the equipment companies and golf shops in the process. Off-course retailers began to proliferate, and they provided additional buying options for players as well as alternative places of employment for PGA Professionals. Then, of course, there was the emergence of Tiger Woods. He turned professional in 1996 after winning his third consecutive U.S. Amateur and the following spring captured his first Masters. His victory at Augusta National was transformational, due to his remarkable skills as a player, of course, and also to his being a young man of multiethnic descent. Through his presence and his play, he put a whole new face on golf and began attracting entirely different demographic groups to the game.

There was a sense at that time that golf had it all going on, and nothing made that more apparent than the Association selling the PGA Merchandise Show to Reed Exhibitions in 1998. It was a smart, strategic move for the PGA, but it was a bellwether, too, signifying to some industry observers that golf was peaking and that many of those involved in the game were so caught up in its progress and popularity that they had started to lose perspective.

Things did head south before too long, beginning with the bursting of the dot-com bubble at the start of the 21st century and then the terrorist attacks of September 11. The economic downturn that followed those events exacerbated what had clearly become an overcapacity not only in golf course inventory but also in club and ball manufacturing. Course construction ground to a halt, and a number of equipment makers downsized dramatically or went out of business. Things only got worse with the arrival of the Great Recession in 2008, and suddenly

PREVIOUS PAGE Jack Nicklaus made his 37th and final appearance in a PGA Championship in 2000 at Valhalla Golf Club, where he was paired with eventual champion Tiger Woods. OPPOSITE Tiger Woods holds the Wanamaker Trophy following his victory at the 2006 PGA Championship, the third of his four PGA Championship titles.

the aspirational middle and upper middle classes that had sustained golf so well had less time and means to keep playing the game as they had years before. The difficult economy also prevented a lot of retirees from teeing it up as much as they had hoped. In addition, the traditional golf and country club models started to break down, as youngsters gravitated more toward team sports that were played primarily on weekends, their parents driving them incessantly from hockey rink to soccer field during the warmer months instead of to the golf course and driving range of their favorite club or facility. Not surprisingly, the game suffered as a result.

There was good news, of course, with the ascension of Suzy Whaley to secretary of the PGA and the eventuality of her becoming the Association's first female president. The quality and performance attributes of the golf equipment being made available to players has never been higher, and the advent of club fitting not only helped golfers enjoy their games more but also gave new importance to the role of the PGA Professional, as well as another reason for people to seek him or her out. The growing prominence of the sort of site-driven golf course development by visionaries like Mike Keiser, Dick Youngscap, and Herb Kohler and the creation of extraordinary new layouts by veterans such as Pete Dye, Robert Trent Jones II, and Tom Fazio and the next generation of golf artists including Bill Coore and Ben Crenshaw, David McLay Kidd, Gil Hanse, and Tom Doak provided players with an embarrassment of architectural riches, as did all the renovation work that the game's best designers were performing on some of the nation's oldest and most celebrated tracks. Never had there been so many good courses for so many people to play, and the state of the competitive game remained formidable with the emergence of bright young stars like Rory McIlroy, Jordan Spieth, Jason Day,

ABOVE Herb Kohler developed the acclaimed Whistling Straits course in Wisconsin, site of the 2004, 2010, and 2015 PGA Championships and 2020 Ryder Cup. OPPOSITE Mike Keiser is one of golf's most respected developers and the visionary behind "pure golf" experiences including Bandon Dunes in Oregon, Cabot Links in Nova Scotia, and Sand Valley in Wisconsin. His model transforms under-utilized land in picturesque and remote locations into must-see golf destinations.

The creation of exceptional new golf courses by veteran designers such as Pete Dye, Robert Trent Jones II, and Tom Fazio, *opposite, clockwise from top left*, and the next generation of artists including, *clockwise from top left*, David McLay Kidd, Gil Hanse, Tom Doak, and Bill Coore and Ben Crenshaw have provided players with modern architectural riches.

Rickie Fowler, Michelle Wie, Stacy Lewis, Lydia Ko, and Lexi Thompson, among others.

Tough as things have been at times in recent years, the game of golf and the people who play it have rarely had it better. That is also the case with the PGA of America, which enters its second century stronger than at any other time in its history, and its professionals, who continue to build and quite ably serve the sport that they love.

Among those who are serving the game so very well is Brendan Walsh. A native of Philadelphia who currently works as the head professional at The Country Club in Brookline, Massachusetts, Walsh was one of 15 children who grew up enjoying the summer sporting life at the Philadelphia Country Club (PCC). His father, William, was an avid golfer, and a good one at that, winning seven club championships at the PCC as well as the Golf Association of Philadelphia Senior Championship when he was 69. As such, it was quite natural for the seven Walsh boys to be attracted to the royal and ancient game. As for the eight sisters, their focus when it came to recreation was swimming, and six of them ended up competing at the national level.

Brendan came into the game when he was five years old and developed into a solid junior player at PCC. It was there that head professional Tom Wilcox began to mentor the young Walsh, encouraging him to attend his alma mater, the College of Wooster, in Ohio. Walsh decided to do so, and shortly after he arrived on campus, he met the school's golf coach, Bob Nye.

Looking back on his college years, Walsh recalls how Nye inspired him to devote more time to golf. The coach also made the game an enjoyable, year-round endeavor, which was something that Walsh, as a talented multisport athlete, had never experienced before. Up to that point, golf had always been a spring sport for Walsh, with football and basketball filling the rest of the year's athletic schedule. Under Coach Nye, however, Walsh participated in daily fall sessions of golf practice and instruction followed by intense winter workouts and conditioning and then an early kickoff of the season with a competitive spring swing through the South.

Walsh followed a small legion of prior players who were also given the opportunity to learn the service and business side of the golf by working for Nye at the college's 9-hole course. He also gained experience on the private club side by laboring under golf team alumnus and former All-American Gary Welshhans at the nearby Wooster Country Club.

While back home in the Philadelphia area for his summers, Walsh caddied at Radnor Valley Country Club in nearby Villanova and at Merion Golf Club. He also looped occasionally at his home club. Following his graduation from college, Walsh took a summer position at Sankaty Head Golf Club in Nantucket, Massachusetts, and then a full-time job at the Ridgewood Country Club near Paramus, New Jersey, spending the next five years at that 27-hole retreat.

"Those jobs gave me the opportunity to experience all aspects of the golf operation," Walsh recalls. "They gave me a lot of confidence that I could be a successful golf professional. They were very supportive of helping us along, giving us every opportunity to succeed. Some people would look at that as you having so much responsibility and duty that you never get a chance to do a lot of things [in your personal life], but I loved it, and I wanted the opportunity to succeed and become a head professional as soon as I could."

OPPOSITE United States Ryder Cup Captain Ben Crenshaw in 1999 at The Country Club in Brookline, Massachusetts, following the historic rally by America over Europe.

With Ridgewood head professional Bill Adams's encouragement, Walsh began applying for a few head professional openings. Among those was the Patterson Club in Fairfield, Connecticut, and the leaders of that facility offered him the job in the fall of 1990. He was only 27 years old. Seven years later, he accepted an even bigger position, as the head professional at The Country Club in Brookline, Massachusetts. For Walsh, it was a dream come true.

At The Country Club, Walsh was following in the footsteps of tenured professional Don Callahan. Callahan had amassed a remarkable reputation over the years, having been a longtime assistant to Claude Harmon at both Winged Foot and Thunderbird Country Club before taking the prestigious Brookline position in 1967. He spent his next 32 years working there. In an unusual yet wise move, The Country Club retained Callahan for two years after hiring Walsh. Callahan was positioned as the club's director of golf and also played a supporting role for Walsh to ensure a smooth transition. They worked side by side through the successful staging of the 1999 Ryder Cup.

In speaking of Callahan, Walsh says, "If you look up the definition of gentleman in the dictionary, you would see a picture of Don there. The way he conducted himself and the respect he had for and from the membership. He loved the game and was wonderful with the members. I had a good role model in Don, and he gave me a real good understanding of what the club was about and how to handle certain situations."

As a product of great mentoring, Walsh offers one important piece of advice Bill Adams taught him. "Don't be afraid to fail," he says. "When you are a head professional in a new position you need to spend the first year or two doing everything, learning every facet of your new operation. After that you have the experience to start delegating some of those responsibilities."

Walsh offers a few clues to his success with his assistants: "Provide them with golf clubs, provide them with equipment, and provide them with a clothing allowance," Walsh explains. "It is going to cost you a few extra dollars but you have to keep them happy. If you keep them happy, and they are being educated and getting better, they are going to work hard for you. If you don't care for your people or treat them with respect, they are not going to perform well. Then your job is going to be in jeopardy."

Walsh also outlines how important it is to assure your assistants are playing the game. "Encourage playing golf, which we have lost a lot in our business. People [golf professionals] aren't playing as much as they used to. They are not driving in their staff as much to get out there and take pride in what the game looks like. That is something we talk about every day. If they are not coming in until 10 a.m., they should be working on their game from 8 to 10 a.m."

When Walsh arrived at The Country Club, he had inherited three skilled assistant professionals who were trained under Callahan. According to Walsh, all three wanted to stay through the Ryder Cup, but he felt he needed to lay down some rules and guidelines to assure success. So, he offered a three-point mission statement for the operation: (1) work as a team, (2) respect one another, and (3) exceed member-guest expectations within the boundaries of the rules. He also requires his team members to create a personal mission statement, suggesting: "Make the most out of yourself each and every day. Make yourself better, whether it is playing more golf, working out, being a better father or a better husband, go to church. Whatever you can do to make yourself a better person every

day . . . be disciplined!" Following the 1999 Ryder Cup all three assistants were able to secure head professional positions.

At the beginning of the 2000 season, Walsh had to completely rebuild his team. In speaking about his interviewing process, he says he always poses one key question: "Do you enjoy doing nice things for people?" If the answer is yes, he follows up with this qualifying question: "Give me three examples in the last thirty days where you have exceeded someone's expectations."

In 2013, Walsh served as the host professional for the U.S. Amateur, awarded to the facility as part of the 100th Anniversary celebration recognizing the club's one-time caddie Francis Ouimet's amazing victory at this historic site in the U.S. Open a century before. Ouimet's childhood home is still standing at 246 Clyde Street, immediately across the street from the course, and it serves as a great reminder of the history that has been made on those special grounds. Walsh says he feels lucky to be a part

of it all and to be a part of the game his father introduced to him so many years ago.

Walsh also says that he is lucky to have worked with so many good assistants in his career, like Jennifer Webster O'Connor, who was part of his team at The Country Club for three years. "She came in with both performance and personality," he says. "She's a bright gal, great with people, a good player and teacher. She could do it all when she first arrived here. Jen is as talented as they get, and she drove herself hard every day."

Webster was born in Mesa, Arizona, and her family moved to Virginia for a few years before settling down in Peabody, Massachusetts. She was six when her parents introduced her to golf. A few years after that, they divorced, and in time, her mother got remarried, to a golf professional named Chris Costa. "That really gave me an opportunity to learn the game," Webster recalls. "I became an addict."

Her subsequent summers became a special time for her, as she would get dropped off at the Massachusetts facility where her stepfather worked, the Middleton Golf Course, and spend the day there. She often started with a round of golf on the 18-hole, par-3 course, followed by a pickup of the practice range before lunch, and then back onto the course in the afternoon. This became an almost everyday schedule. "I went a couple of summers where I played nonstop," she says.

A love of basketball prevented Webster from indulging in more than a limited amount of competitive golf before going into high school, but no one would have known that from the way she played. In her freshman year, she finished second in the Massachusetts Girls' High School Championship. Then she captured the

---

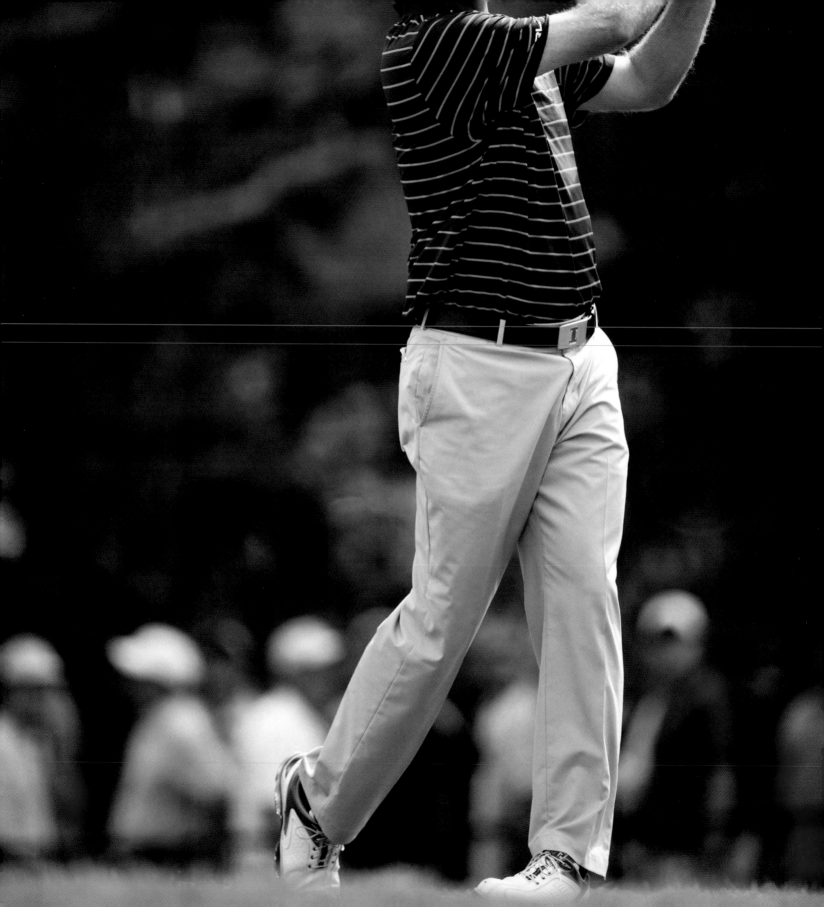

Massachusetts Girls' High School title in her sophomore and junior years. As a senior, Webster finished second again.

When it came time for college, she went to Drexel University in Philadelphia on a basketball scholarship. As a result, she all but stopped teeing it competitively. She earned an undergraduate degree at Drexel, and then an MBA from the same school, fielding a slew of job offers from Wall Street firms when her studies were finished. She decided to pursue a career in golf instead.

Webster started as an assistant at Glastonbury Hills in Connecticut, after which she moved to Fox Hopyard to work as first assistant to Ron Beck. Then, in 2004, she joined Walsh's staff, where she spent a total of three years at Brookline, the final two as his first assistant. At that point, it was time for her to begin searching for her first head position. Although she had a number of solid opportunities, one facility stood out, Prouts Neck Country Club, just south of Portland, Maine. "It gave me the opportunity to run my own business, which was consistent with my goals coming out of school," she says.

Her position at Prouts Neck was seasonal, and that allowed Webster to follow another side of her teaching passion. So, in 2007, she joined the PGA Education Adjunct Faculty teaching in the Professional Golf Management (PGM) Program at accredited PGA Golf Management University Programs and in Port St. Lucie, Florida at the PGA Education Center. She acknowledges that the academic world has always been a comfortable place for her, so it seemed like a natural fit.

One of the greatest benefits of being a part of that group is learning from the full-time PGA faculty and the other talented professionals who are also offering their time and experiences to improve the education process. Along the way Webster met and worked with one of the Minnesota Section's outstanding professionals, Joe O'Connor.

After an assistantship at Edina Country Club in suburban Minneapolis, O'Connor moved up as the head professional at Duluth, Minnesota's Northland Country Club in 1988. Success followed him, and he remained in that position through 2010, before becoming the club's PGA general manager in 2011.

When O'Connor was being elevated to the GM position at Northland, he knew the perfect candidate to replace him as head professional: Jennifer Webster. He approached the club's board with his candidate, lauding her qualities as a golf professional. After taking his recommendation under consideration, the club's president reviewed Webster's résumé, thanked O'Connor for the recommendation, and then invited Webster to fly out to Duluth to spend a day with the club's board. After a review of her credentials, a successful interview, and an examination of potential consequences of the relationship with O'Connor, club leaders offered Webster the job. That was in the fall of 2010, and three years later, Webster and O'Connor married. Today, they make up that rare tandem of PGA husband and wife and GM and head professional, married to the game of golf and to each other

There is a growing trend in the PGA of America of husband-and-wife members. One such example is Matt and Jennifer Borocz, who work in Florida. Matt is the director of golf and assistant general manager at the TPC Sawgrass in Ponte Vedra, while Jennifer serves as the women's golf coach for nearby Jacksonville University. In many ways, theirs is a match made in golf heaven.

Matt Borocz was born in Strongsville, Ohio, growing up in a family where his father, grandfather, and brother played golf. Mostly, they teed it at a daily fee track called Pine Hills, and one thing Borocz clearly remembers was his attraction to the pro shop, which was one of the best in the area. "I liked nice clothes," he says, "and they featured Ashworth shirts." When he wasn't out on the course or practicing, Borocz liked to hang around the pro shop. The facility's PGA Professional was Steve Brzytwa, and he soon offered Borocz a job picking up balls on the practice range in return for free golf and the occasional sleeve of new golf balls. Of course, Borocz accepted, and the game seeped so deeply into his soul that he knew by the time he entered high school that he wanted to make golf a career.

Borocz still felt that way when it was time to look at colleges, and that was why he was interested in Coastal Carolina, which had just started a PGM Program. It also had the added benefit of being a great golf area, located as it was near Myrtle Beach. Borocz liked what he saw when he visited the college campus and was especially intrigued by a billboard he espied announcing the construction of the new TPC Myrtle Beach, thinking to himself, "Wouldn't it be cool to work there one day?"

Borocz soon began his studies at Coastal Carolina and after one semester applied for a job at TPC Myrtle Beach. Within a month of submitting his application, he was employed there as a practice facility attendant as he also studied at his new school. He could not have been happier.

Borocz stayed at TPC Myrtle Beach even after graduating from Coastal Carolina, rising all the way to senior assistant PGA Professional. Then, in 2004, he moved to TPC Sawgrass, arriving just two weeks before The Players Championship

that year. His first task was to manage the golf shop during tournament week, and then he went on to serve as an assistant for the bustling operation.

Less than two years later, Jim Poole, the club's head professional, left for another job opportunity. The organization decided to consider Borocz as Poole's replacement, and after watching him help lead a massive renovation effort of both the Stadium Course at TPC Sawgrass and the replacement of the original, pyramid-shaped clubhouse with a 100,000-square-foot structure, they named him head professional. In August 2013, after six successful years in that position, the club promoted Borocz to director of golf/assistant general manager. "I love golf and I enjoy learning what goes on in other departments," Borocz says. "As a result, I have enjoyed the new position immensely because I have been able to work with food and beverage, golf course maintenance, sales and marketing, accounting, PGA Tour headquarters, and the Players Championship pieces."

As head professional at TPC Sawgrass, Borocz had determined that he was going to create one of the finest PGM intern experiences for potential PGA members in the land, and some 60 young men and women have worked over the years as interns at TPC Sawgrass. One of those came to TPC Sawgrass from Minnesota, where she had been working at TPC Twin Cities, and she must have made quite an impression, for she and Borocz eventually started dating. Three years after they met, they married.

Jennifer Heinz Borocz took up golf when she was 11 years old and competed on the girl's high school golf team. She went to Sam Houston State University to play golf and also to study nursing, but after working a couple of summers at a local golf course in the Twin Cities,

she decide to change things up and pursue a degree in general business management with a PGM minor. She became a member of the PGA in 2009, and that same year she started work at TPC Sawgrass as an intern, serving for a while as tournament manager. She did well in that role and clearly had a big future there, but as her relationship with Borocz started to blossom, they knew they could no longer work at the same facility, so Jennifer Heinz Borocz left TPC Sawgrass. Fortune quickly smiled on her as she learned that Jacksonville University was looking for a full-time women's golf coach. The school interviewed her and then hired her.

Somehow between their two jobs, Jennifer and Matt managed to start a family, and they now have a young son named Carter, who frequently spends time around his father at TPC Sawgrass and occasionally accompanies his mother's squad to tournaments. Even at a very young age, Carter has become immersed in the game, and one of his favorite phrases is "I love daddy, mommy, and the girls." Clearly, he also loves golf.

So, too, does Mary Beth Nienhaus, even though golf came to her as much by proximity as intent when she grew up on Maple Street in Appleton, Wisconsin, directly across the street from Reid Golf Course. Nienhaus received her first set of clubs when she was only 6 years old, and by the time she was 12, she was playing and practicing daily, concentrating on developing her game and leaving other warm-season sports behind. At 15, she won her first Appleton City Championship.

Nienhaus enrolled at Marquette University in Milwaukee, Wisconsin, in 1963, and that summer she won in the Wisconsin Women's Public Links Association Amateur Championship. Dr. Charles Nader, a Marquette physical education professor and men's golf coach, invited her to play for his team when she returned to classes. The invitation was significant because it made her the university's first female intercollegiate athlete in any sport.

Following college, Nienhaus continued to play competitively, adding several other titles to her golf résumé, including the Wisconsin Women's State Golf Association (WWSGA) Amateur Championship in 1968 and 1969. In 1969, she was named the Wisconsin Female Golfer of the Year. The following year, she was elected president of the WWSGA.

As a mathematics major and physical education minor, Nienhaus found work teaching physical education at Kaukauna High School, which was only 10 miles from her hometown of Appleton. After four years there, Nienhaus returned to college to earn a master's degree in education from Illinois State University. Advanced degree in hand, she found a physical education position at Appleton West High School in 1971. In that same year, she gave up her amateur status to turn professional and began teaching golf summers at Winagamie Golf Course, a privately owned public facility in neighboring Neenah.

Over her high school coaching career, Nienhaus proved to be an extremely versatile individual. Her golf teams earned four state championships and produced three state medalists. She also coached basketball and volleyball as well as gymnastics, cheerleading, and track. In 1987, she was recognized by the national LPGA with their Coach of the Year award, and she remains the only high school coach ever among its recipients.

After Nienhaus's first year at Winagamie, she took out a loan to become the fifth partner. At the same time, she was named the course manager and golf professional. Over the next 20 years, she was able to buy out her partners to become

OPPOSITE Ralph Landrum has epitomized what growing the game with passion and creativity means in today's golf industry. The PGA general manager at The World of Golf in Florence, Kentucky, was honored with the 2014 PGA Player Development Award.

the sole owner. Once that happened, Nienhaus set into motion a long-term plan to improve overall operations. Her first agenda item was the replacement of the original irrigation system installed when the course opened in 1962. Then, she retired from teaching and coaching after a remarkable career that spanned 33 years so she could devote all her time to Winagamie. In time, Nienhaus brought in the PGA Tour Design Services to expand the facility to 27 holes. Soon after, she renovated the clubhouse. "Through the years, I put a lot of time and energy and money into the golf course because I wanted to make it one of the better facilities in the area," she says. "I think we accomplished that."

A LPGA Master Life Professional, Nienhaus also created a junior program that extended to a number of communities in her multicounty area. Through her summer instruction offerings, tournaments, and outreach to local school systems and youth organizations, Nienhaus introduced the game to thousands of students each year. In fact, it became a common sight at Winagamie to see yellow school buses filled with children pulling into the parking lot for their introduction to the game. "Our mission was for children to learn life skills while we are teaching golf skills to them," Nienhaus said.

In 1997, she surprised her hometown community with a gift of $200,000 to a local education foundation to renovate abandoned sports fields. It is now known as the Nienhaus Sports Complex. Then, in 2011, she stepped forward with another gift, this time in the amount of $100,000, for the Appleton West High School's "Addition to Tradition" project.

As she neared retirement age, Nienhaus began to consider her future, as well as the years ahead for Winagamie Golf Course and her youth programs. Wanting to ensure her work would continue, and in a truly unique move for education, she made the extraordinary gift of the 27-hole facility to the Appleton Education Foundation in 2014. It was just one more example of Nienhaus giving back to the game she has loved for so long.

Suzy Whaley has also given a great deal to golf, and she has received well-deserved accolades for the ways she has worked for the national and Section offices of the PGA and assisted the Association in its grow-the-game outreach programs for women and youth, however it was her playing that first got her noticed. A graduate of the University of North Carolina, where she majored in economics, Whaley competed for a couple of years on the LPGA Tour after graduating then she moved to Connecticut, where she won three state Women's Opens. Winning the PGA Section Championship in 2002 compelled people to suddenly consider her competitive skills, and achieving that earned Whaley a spot in the 2003 Greater Hartford Open and the distinction of becoming the first woman in 58 years to qualify for a PGA Tour event.

As good a victory as it was for her, winning that Section Championship created something of a difficult situation for the PGA of America and the PGA Tour. As a woman, she had been granted the standard 10 percent yardage advantage over the field in that event, meaning that while her male competitors played the Ellington Ridge Country Club at 6,938 yards, Whaley teed it from 6,244 yards, delivering rounds of 68-72-71. The question being pondered most often was, in what manner, if any, would her tee placement play a role in her qualification to a PGA Tour event where she obviously would not be granted any such adjustment?

OPPOSITE Suzy Whaley of Farmington, Connecticut, was the first woman elected to serve as an officer of the PGA of America, a milestone she preceded by achieving a series of "firsts" as a competitive player.

The local PGA Tour event, then the Greater Hartford Open, was quick to react when PGA member and tournament director Dan Baker stated: "Whaley distinguished herself as a player, and we'd be thrilled to have her. She's a great player. She earned it." The PGA Tour responded to the controversy through spokesman Bob Combs: "The rules of competition are established by the local Section of the PGA of America, and whatever they set up we accept. As far as we are concerned, there's a spot in the GHO with her name on it."

The news of her victory, more specifically her entry into the Greater Hartford Open, made international headlines. Hundreds of phone calls and requests for interviews flooded in as Whaley considered whether or not she would accept the exemption. Eventually, she chose to compete, playing from the same tees as the men and missing the cut as she posted rounds of 75 and 78.

At the time, Whaley was the head professional at Blue Fox Run Golf Course in Avon, Connecticut, and she parlayed her newfound notoriety, and recognition, in a number of ways. For two years, from 2004 to 2006, she served as a commentator on the LPGA Tour for ESPN. She also went to work as the director of instruction at TPC River Highlands in Cromwell, which has been the longtime site of the Hartford tournament. In later years, she founded Suzy Whaley Golf at that locale and became its director of instruction. She received a variety of honors for her teaching prowess, including being selected as one of *Golf Digest*'s 50 Best Teachers and twice receiving the Connecticut PGA Section's Teacher of the Year award.

Over the next decade, Whaley became increasingly active in the PGA, and in 2014, Association members elected her to be their secretary. That made her the first woman to be a national officer of the Association and put her in line to ascend to the PGA presidency in 2018. Still breaking new ground in golf, and still giving back.

Many of the Professionals that PGA officers like Suzy Whaley represent have relatively traditional jobs that entail giving lessons, competing in their Section tournaments, running member-guest tournaments, and selling clubs and apparel out of their pro shops, but as modern PGA members well know, their work these days can entail other duties. Some have become involved in resort management or golf real estate development, for example, while others have gotten into coaching. A few have been known to work for golf equipment companies in different capacities, and there are no shortage of men and women of the PGA who have gone on to serve their places of businesses as general managers and even golf course superintendents. The possibilities, in many ways, are endless.

Consider Dana Garmany. First and foremost, he wanted to be a golfer, but the PGA Professional with the University of Alabama degree has ended up making his living in the game in an entirely different manner, that as the chairman and chief executive of Troon Golf, which is today regarded as the largest third-party manager of golf and club operations in the world.

It started in 1990, when Garmany founded Scottsdale, Arizona-based Troon Golf with developer Jerry Nelson. "I definitely felt that daily-fee resort golf was treated as a little brother to private clubs," says Garmany, "and I clearly believed there was an opportunity to make that experience better and more positive. However, my dreams were quite small compared to where things ended up. At first, I remember hoping to have 10 golf courses under management one day, and now, over 240, with a full one-third of them private, the remaining split between daily-fee, resort, and semiprivate."

Troon Golf currently employs more than 350 PGA Professionals, and all told, some 10,000 people in 26 countries and 31 states work for the operation. Its portfolio of properties includes the Boulders and the Phoenician in Arizona, PGA West in Southern California, and Kapalua in Hawaii. That is an expansive list, and Garmany says there are plenty of opportunities out there for Professionals who can think bigger and bolder. "The PGA member is now in an ideal position to be, say, the GM of most places, if they have that desire," he says. "Never has there been a bigger opportunity for dreamers and aggressive thinkers."

There are opportunities for teachers and course operators, too, and few Association members have mined those realms more completely than Master Professional Ralph Landrum. A former PGA Tour professional, he runs the World of Golf in Crestview Hills, Kentucky, and his receipt of the 2014 PGA Player Development Award for extraordinary contributions in growing the game is an indication of how highly he is regarded as an instructor.

Early in his career, Landrum was some kind of player, finishing eighth in the 1983 U.S. Open, but in 1985 he left the PGA Tour to begin operating golf courses. His goal, he says, has long been to enhance golf opportunities for all players, most especially juniors and women. To help achieve that, Landrum has taught tirelessly, and he estimates that he gave more than 1,000 lessons in 2014 alone. He has also served on the national PGA Growth of the Game Committee and implemented numerous player development programs in his work.

Ira McGraw Jr. is also a mentor of note. The owner of IAMJ Enterprises Inc., he is the general manager and director of golf at Cedar Crest Golf Course in Dallas, Texas, as well as a beacon to inner-city youth through the First Tee of Greater Dallas.

To appreciate the things McGraw has done for golf and golfers in his career, one needs only to hear the story of Lester Bell, to whom McGraw and his wife, Yesenia, are now legal guardians. For many years, Bell lived in poverty and unsafe conditions at home. Then, at the age of 13, he developed a love for golf as he built a bond with McGraw. Like a script drawn from the hit movie *The Blind Side*, McGraw and Yesenia accepted Bell into their family and guided him toward a college education at Texas Southern University. On his way, Bell became captain of his high school golf team. "I played golf with my mom growing up at Cedar Crest and I pass places on the course all the time that is a memory, and whenever this happens, I am humbled all over again," says McGraw. "When we work with some of the kids, I just can't help but see a bit of myself in them. My feeling this way is what initiated my relationship with Lester."

McGraw attended Southern University and A&M College in Baton Rouge, Louisiana, and furthered his education at Amberton University in Dallas, Texas, before attaining PGA membership in 2007. The next year, McGraw was awarded the management contract at Cedar Crest Golf Course in Dallas. He is now a member of the board of directors of the Northern Texas PGA Section and donates countless summer hours to working with young people in his community. By his count, he has introduced golf to and coached more than 800 inner-city youths. "Some of these kids need so much, and I feel it is part of my responsibility at this facility to be a part of the community and to be an example and role model for kids to look up to," he says.

OPPOSITE Jordan Spieth delivered a jolt of excitement to professional golf in 2015 by nearly achieving the elusive Grand Slam and bringing new fans to the game.

really is more than golf, its life. My wife and I really felt that we were given an opportunity to impact a person's life. We all do things to help people all the time, whether it is a family member or a friend or friend of a friend. I can't imagine being faced with that great opportunity and turning my back."

Of course, coaching is a form of mentoring, and Mike Small of the University of Illinois has done a superb job of that. A 1988 graduate of that institution, he returned to his alma mater in 2000 to lead the golf team after a less than satisfactory attempt to make it on the PGA Tour. In the 15 years since, he has proved himself to be a formidable coach, guiding the Fighting Illini to six Big Ten Conference Championships during that time as well as eight consecutive NCAA Championship appearances and three straight NCAA Regional titles. His 2012–13 team was an NCAA runner-up; and in 2014–15, Illinois had a school-record eight tournament titles. Small added to his seven Big Ten coaching honors by being selected the 2015 National Coach of the Year by the Golf Coaches Association of America.

Wedged in his year-round work as a Division I coach and the responsibilities of recruiting and managing young athletes, Small somehow managed to become the most successful playing college coach in PGA history, proving that he did not give up his dreams as a competitive golfer when he decided to become a coach. He won PGA Professional National Championships in 2005, '09, and '10, garnered three PGA Professional Player of the Year Awards, and competed on five PGA Cup teams, which is the equivalent of the Ryder Cup for the club professional. A member of the Illinois Golf Hall of Fame, Small has won a record 11 Illinois PGA Championships and four

Illinois Opens. "To become a PGA of America member, to continue to play events, which is who I am, and then coach, well, it was an unbelievable opportunity for me," says Small. "Not only did my career expand, but my life expanded."

The same has held true for Gene Mattare, and one of the things he always liked best about being a PGA Professional was that it gave him the chance to perform a variety of tasks in his job, such as teaching, for example, as well as playing and merchandising. The Washington, DC, native with a B.A. in psychology from George Washington University has a facile mind and a multitude of interests.

Quite frankly, he would have been bored in a job that did not afford him the opportunities to learn and grow, so Mattare embraced all that golf gave him. He served for four years as the men's varsity golf team coach at his college alma mater and then worked for four years as the assistant golf professional at the Chevy Chase Club in Chevy Chase, Maryland. In 1981, he assumed the top position at the Princess Anne Country Club in Virginia, staying there for 10 years before leaders at the Saucon Valley Country Club in Bethlehem, Pennsylvania, hired him to be their head professional. It was a position that certainly kept Mattare occupied, as Saucon boasts a trio of golf courses, two golf shops, and 11 restaurants.

After 14 years in that role, Mattare was ready to take on even more, so he became the club's general manager, adding those duties to the ones he was already performing as director of golf. He says he enjoys the additional responsibilities that came with that new assignment and relishes the say he has in how the entire club is run. "It's been wonderful being the director of golf at Saucon Valley," Mattare says. "It's been even better having the job as general manager as well."

AFTERWORD *by Annika Sörenstam, PGA*

I can sort of imagine how the immigrant golf professionals who came to America in the late 1800s and early 1900s felt. They crossed a great ocean to start a new life in the New World; generations later, I embarked on somewhat of a similar journey, as a teenager from Sweden ready to explore the challenges of golf in the United States. The big difference, of course, is that while I was concentrating on being a competitive player, those courageous travelers of yesteryear were also tasked with teaching golf to an entire nation and showing an enthusiastic but inexperienced public what the royal and ancient game was all about. They came here to work and play tournaments but also to spread the gospel of golf.

From the very beginning, golf professionals in America have focused on promoting and growing the game. That mission took on new meaning and focus in 1916, when several of the most prominent members of that fraternity founded the PGA of America. In the 100 years since the Association started, those men and women have worked hard to make it one of the most popular—and most-played—sports in the United States.

I was elected to PGA membership two years ago, and I take enormous pride in being a part of the organization. The men and women professionals who comprise the Association are tireless caretakers, nurturers, and promoters of golf, and I respect their passion to elevate their profession.

The PGA Professionals I have met and worked with over the years take their heritage very seriously. They appreciate how important it is to teach the values and pleasures of golf as they perform the everyday duties of teaching the swing, explaining the rules that govern the game, running member tournaments, and selling merchandise and equipment. I have used the tagline "Share My Passion" for my businesses and for my life in general, but I also see it as a guiding force for golf professionals today.

Golf is in a good place as we celebrate the PGA of America's centennial, and that is thanks in many ways to the great men and women members of that group. Their broad skillsets are matched only by their energy and desire to help the next generation of golfers learn and love the game. They see that as integral to their mission and also as a way of giving back and paying tribute to those professionals who came before them, and I believe that wherever golf may take us in the next century, we will find PGA Professionals helping lead the way.

Congratulations to the PGA of America and its 28,000 members. You are among golf's Most Valuable Players, and we thank you for rising each day to provide a new level of enjoyment to this wonderful game.

OPPOSITE After retiring from competition in 2008 following one of the greatest careers in women's golf history, PGA Professional Annika Sörenstam has become a golf business leader and an inspiration to a new generation of golfers.

January 17th 1916.

A number of Golf Professionals were invited to luncheon at the Taplow Club by Mr Rodman Wannamaker.

The object of this gathering of Professionals was to discuss the feasability of forming a national Assn of Prof. Golfers similar to the P.G.A. of Gt Britian, several prominent amateurs were present, and amongst those who spoke in favor of organizing were

Mr Francis Quimet
Mr John G. Anderson
Mr A. W. Tillinghast
Mr Joseph Appel
Mr W. W. Harris
Mr P. C. Pulver
Mr Jason Rogers

Mr Rodman Wannamaker Kindly offered to donate prizes for a Tournament to be run on lines similar to the News of World.

An organizing Committee was Appointed as follows:-

James Hepburn. Chair
James Maiden
Robt White
Gilbert Nicholls
Jack Mackie
Jack Hobens
Herbert Strong   Sec.

Enrolled as Charter Members attached

January 17th 1916

A meeting of the Organizing Committee was held at three P.M. It was decided that a meeting be called for Monday Jan 24th at 12.30 to discuss methods of drawing up constitution and bye-laws and that the following gentlemen be invited to attend this meeting.

Mr. W. C. Freeman
Mr. F. C. Ennever
Mr. W. W. Harris
Mr. Jason Rogers
Mr. P. C. Pulver

Meeting adjourned 4 P.M.

January 24th 1916.

A meeting of the Organizing Committee was held at the Toplow Club; suggestions were offered for drawing up constitution & bye-laws by Mr. W. C. Freeman, Mr. F. C. Ennever, Mr. Jason Rogers, and Mr. P. C. Pulver. It was decided to wait until a copy of the constitution & bye-laws from Gt. Britian arrived. Mr. Jason Rogers kindly offered his services to the Committee relative to drawing up said constitution. Meeting adjourned 2.30 P.M.

Feb 7th 1916. Martinique Hotel

Meeting of Organizing Com. was called to order at 1 P.M. minutes of previous meeting was accepted as read.

Motion made & seconded that we proceed to organize.

Motion carried unanimously.

1916

- Nearly 60 golf professionals and leading amateurs are invited to a luncheon, January 17, in the Wanamaker Store in New York City. Department store magnate Rodman Wanamaker, the luncheon host, believes golf professionals may enhance their business prospects by forming an association.
- On April 10, the Professional Golfers' Association of America is founded with 35 charter members in the second-floor boardroom of the Hotel Martinique on 32nd and Broadway in New York City.
- The first Organizing Annual Meeting is held June 26, at the Radisson Hotel in Minneapolis, Minnesota.
- The inaugural PGA Championship is conducted, October 10–14, in a match play format at Siwanoy Country Club in Bronxville, New York. Jim Barnes defeats Jock Hutchison, 1 up, in the Championship match.
- The U.S. Golf Association extends the PGA of America the privilege of choosing the host club for the 1917 U.S. Open. Whitemarsh Valley Country Club is selected.

1917

- The PGA Championship is canceled due to World War I.
- The Association contacts clubs about holding positions open for PGA members in the armed forces.
- The PGA of America purchases an ambulance for the Red Cross and votes to maintain it until the end of the war.

1918

- The PGA of America votes to send $1,000 to the British PGA for war relief.
- The PGA Championship again canceled due to World War I.

1919

- The PGA Championship resumes, and Jim Barnes successfully defends his title. with a 6 and 5 victory over Fred McLeod at Engineers Country Club in Roslyn, New York.

1920

- The first issue of The Professional Golfer of America is published in May by the PGA, with P. C. Pulver named editor.

1921

- Walter Hagen becomes the first American-born PGA Champion, defeating two-time winner Jim Barnes, 3 and 2, at Linwood Country Club in Far Rockaway, New York.
- Jock Hutchison, a native of St. Andrews, Scotland, returns to his hometown and becomes the first American citizen to win the Open Championship.

1922

- Manufacturers advise that $3 should be the maximum price for a PGA line of irons.
- Gene Sarazen wins his first PGA Championship at the age of 20.
- Walter Hagen becomes the first American-born golfer to win the Open Championship. The USGA adopts the suggestion of the PGA to play the U.S. Open annually in June.

1923

- At its Annual Meeting, the PGA recommends that all PGA steel-shafted iron models be stamped "This head approved by the PGA."
- Gene Sarazen wins his second consecutive PGA Championship, defeating Walter Hagen, 1-up, at Pelham Country Club in Pelham Manor, New York.

OPPOSITE Don Perne, *left*, spent many years as a PGA Professional at Inverness Club in Toledo, Ohio, and also helped found the first PGA-sanctioned golf management program at what is today Ferris State University in Big Rapids, Michigan.

1924

- The PGA Champion is exempted from qualifying rounds to the PGA Championship.
- Walter Hagen wins his second PGA Championship, 2 up, over previous two-time champion Jim Barnes.

1925

- An entry fee of $5 is charged for PGA Championship qualifying rounds.
- Official figures show membership in the PGA of America now stands at 1,548.

1926

- Steel shafts are legalized by the USGA.

1927

- The United States defeats Great Britain 9 1/2–2 1/2 in the inaugural Ryder Cup at Worcester Country Club in Worcester, Massachusetts.
- Walter Hagen wins his fifth PGA Championship, his fourth in a row, at Cedar Crest Golf Course in Dallas.

1929

- Steel shafts legalized by Royal and Ancient Golf Club of St. Andrews, Scotland.
- Hal Sharkey named to manage fledgling Tournament Bureau.
- The stock market crash is a forerunner of a worldwide depression.

1930

- The PGA national office moves from New York to Chicago.
- Bobby Jones wins the Grand Slam—the U.S. Open, U.S. Amateur, Open Championship, and British Amateur—and then retires from active competition at age 28.
- The name "PGA" is trademarked and The Professional Golfer of America magazine is copyrighted.
- Tommy Armour becomes third foreign-born PGA Champion.

- The Wanamaker Trophy is found in a warehouse in Chicago after a mysterious disappearance in a taxi hired to bring Walter Hagen's luggage to a hotel a few years earlier.

1933

- George Jacobus becomes the first American-born president of the PGA of America. Jacobus also is the first PGA president to rise from the caddie ranks.
- An article by President Jacobus appears in every issue of The Professional Golfer of America magazine.
- The Association creates an Unemployment Relief Committee as the Great Depression worsens.
- Membership now requires a three-year apprenticeship.

1934

- Horton Smith wins the inaugural Augusta National Invitation Tournament (the Masters) at Augusta National Golf Club in Georgia, posting a 284 for 72 holes.

1935

- Golf course architect A. W. Tillinghast is hired to provide PGA members with consulting service on design of their courses.
- More than 200 PGA members participate in matches against a visiting six-man team from Japan.

1936

- Membership in the PGA of America grows to 1,800.
- The Golf Promotion Bureau, forerunner of the National Golf Foundation, is started as a market development service by Herb and Joe Graffis, publishers of Golfdom.

1937

- The inaugural Senior PGA Championship is hosted by Augusta National Golf Club. Jock Hutchison wins the 54-hole championship with a score of 223, following rounds of 76, 75, and 72.

- The Vardon Trophy is established as a way of recognizing the touring professional with the lowest scoring average. Harry Cooper is the first recipient.

1938
- Judge Earle F. Tilly endows his extensive golf library to the PGA of America.

1939
- The Ryder Cup is canceled due to the outbreak of World War II.

1940
- The Benevolent and Relief Fund pays $4,662 to members unable to work.
- The Unemployment Fund pays $1,085 to members unable to find jobs.
- PGA Sections conduct successful public relations campaign to stop large corporations from buying golf equipment and reselling it to their employees at cost.

1941
- The PGA celebrates its 25th anniversary, with its rolls now containing 2,041 members. The Association also establishes the Golf Hall of Fame. The first inductees are Willie Anderson, Tommy Armour, Jim Barnes, Chick Evans, Walter Hagen, Bobby Jones, John McDermott, Francis Ouimet, Gene Sarazen, Alex Smith, Jerry Travers, and Walter Travis.

1942
- The PGA purchases two ambulances for the Red Cross and distributes clubs and balls at military bases.
- The Association raises more than $25,000 for USO, Red Cross, navy and army Relief.
- The field at the PGA Championship consists of 32 players, the majority of whom are service members on leave.
- Sam Snead wins the first of his three PGA Championships and then reports for U.S. Navy duty the next day.

1943
- The PGA Championship is canceled due to World War II.
- Bob Hope and Bing Crosby play six weeks of exhibition matches with professionals and amateurs to sell war bonds.

1944
- The publication offices of The Professional Golfer of America magazine are moved to Chicago.
- The PGA signs lease with city of Dunedin, Florida, to turn the city course into the PGA National Golf Club.

1945
- The PGA starts rebuilding after the war with 1,565 members.
- The Senior PGA Championship moves to Dunedin, Florida.

1946
- There are 2,236 members in the PGA of America.
- The Golf Writers Association of America is organized at Oregon's Portland Golf Club during the PGA Championship.
- Tournament players reach agreement with the PGA to operate in complete autonomy.

1947
- The Ryder Cup resumes at the Portland Golf Club when Robert Hudson, an Oregon fruit packer, finances the British team's expenses.
- The PGA Championship at Plum Hollow Country Club in Detroit attracts 53,000 spectators, a new attendance record.

1948
- Ben Hogan wins his second and final PGA Championship. A near-fatal automobile accident a few months later prevents him from defending his PGA Championship the next year. Hogan does not compete in the PGA Championship again until 1960.

1949

- The USGA asks the Tournament Bureau to do something about slow play.
- The Quarter Century Club formed for members with 25 years or more in professional golf.

1950

- The Education Committee, headed by Eddie Duino, and the National Golf Foundation publish book on pro-department operations.
- The Teaching Committee, headed by Harold Sargent, issues "A Teacher's Guide."
- The PGA and Junior Chamber of Commerce stage the Jaycee Junior Championship with approximately 10,000 entries.

1951

- Horton Smith elected to his first term as president at the 35th PGA Organizing Annual Meeting.
- The "stymie" is abolished by the Royal and Ancient Golf Club of St. Andrews, Scotland, and the United States Golf Association (USGA).

1952

- The PGA of America, in conjunction with Life magazine, sponsors the first National Golf Day and raises $80,000 for charity.

1953

- Ben Hogan, electing to bypass the PGA Championship and its arduous match play format, wins the Open Championship at Carnoustie, Scotland. The victory gives him three-quarters of the Grand Slam in one year, having previously won the Masters and U.S. Open.

1954

- The PGA Merchandise Show is born in a parking lot at PGA National Golf Club in Dunedin, Florida. Salesmen gather to exhibit their product lines during the Senior PGA Championship.

1955

- The PGA Golf Professional of the Year Award is established to honor a PGA member for total contributions to the game. Bill Gordon, of Tam O'Shanter Country Club in Chicago, is the first recipient.

1956

- The PGA national office moves from Chicago to Dunedin, Florida.
- Membership in the PGA of America reaches 3,798, and the number of PGA Sections expands to 31.

1957

- Lionel Hebert defeats Dow Finsterwald 2 and 1 at Miami Valley Golf Club in Dayton, Ohio, the last PGA Championship conducted at match play.

1958

- PGA Championship changes to a stroke-play format, and 1957 runner-up Dow Finsterwald posts a 4-under-par 276 for the victory.
- Arnold Palmer plays in his first PGA Championship, wins his first Masters, and finishes the year as the Tour's leading money-winner.
- CBS-TV purchases broadcasting rights for the PGA Championship.
- The number of PGA Sections increases to 33, with the additions of the Colorado and Southwest PGA Sections.
- The 40th PGA Championship at Llanerch Country Club in Havertown, Pennsylvania, is the first PGA Championship to be broadcast on live television and radio.

1959

- The Georgia-Alabama Section officially withdraws from the Southeastern Section to become the 34th PGA Section.
- The PGA rents 60-by-180-foot tent for the PGA Merchandise Show during the Senior PGA Championship at Dunedin, Florida.

1961

- The PGA's national offices move from 2,500 square feet on second floor of a bank building in Dunedin, Florida, to larger quarters in town comprising approximately 7,000 square feet.
- Paul Runyan (PGA Champion in 1934 and 1938) wins his first Senior PGA Championship, while Buck White sets a tournament record for the lowest round with an opening 63.

1962

- The PGA sells its holdings in Dunedin Isles Golf Club back to the city for $50,000, in anticipation of move to Florida's east coast.
- Gary Player becomes the fifth foreign-born PGA Champion.

1963

- Jack Nicklaus wins his first PGA Championship.

1964

- The Horton Smith Trophy is donated by the PGA Advisory Committee to recognize an individual member for outstanding contributions to professional education.

1965

- The PGA national headquarters moves from Dunedin, Florida, to Palm Beach Gardens, Florida.
- The PGA of America employs its first director of education.
- Emil Beck, of Port Huron, Michigan, is the first Horton Smith Trophy recipient.

1966

- On its 50th anniversary, membership in the PGA of America stands at 5,837.

1968

- The first PGA Club Professional Championship is held at Century Country Club and Roadrunner Country Club in Scottsdale, Arizona.

- Tournament players form their own organization, the Association of Professional Golfers.
- Tournament players abolish APG and agree to operate as fully autonomous Tournament Players Division (TPD) under supervision of a new 10-member Tournament Policy Board.

1969

- Joseph Dey, executive director of the USGA, is named the new commissioner of the Tournament Players Division

1970

- The PGA of America Apprentice Program is established.
- The PGA Credit Union is established.
- The PGA establishes a Golf Facility Certification Program, with 1,900 certified the first year.

1971

- As part of an agreement to promote winter tourism and the host city, the PGA Championship is played in February at the PGA National Golf Club in Palm Beach Gardens, Florida. Jack Nicklaus captures the Wanamaker Trophy.
- Jack Nicklaus becomes the first professional to win the Masters, U.S. Open, British Open, and PGA Championship twice.

1972

- Gary Player wins his second PGA Championship.
- James D. Fogertey of Kirkwood, Missouri, becomes the first PGA Master Professional.

1973

- The PGA of America moves its offices to Lake Park, Florida.
- The first PGA Cup, modeled after the Ryder Cup and featuring PGA club professionals from the United States and Great Britain, is held at Pinehurst in North Carolina.
- A mandatory Playing Ability Test is adopted for all members.

1974

- Deane Beman succeeds Joseph Dey as commissioner of the Tournament Players Division.

1975

- The Tournament Players Division renamed the PGA Tour.
- A new agreement is signed between the PGA of America and the PGA Tour, creating the World Series of Golf as a joint property.
- The PGA Employment & Club Relations department established.
- The first PGA Golf Management Program is founded at Ferris State University in Big Rapids, Michigan.

1976

- The inaugural Junior PGA Championship held at Walt Disney World Golf resort in Orlando, Florida.

1977

- Mike Zack wins the first PGA Assistant Professional Championship at Thorny Lea Golf Club in Brockton, Massachusetts.

1978

- The PGA Junior Golf Foundation is created to help develop national junior golf programs and initiatives.

1979

- The Bill Strausbaugh Club Relations Award is established to recognize a PGA member for outstanding work in improving employment conditions. The Grand Slam of Golf is created to help raise funds to support the Junior Golf Foundation.
- David Graham becomes the sixth foreign-born PGA Champion.

1980

- Jack Nicklaus wins his fifth PGA Championship, tying Walter Hagen for most Championships won.
- Arnold Palmer wins his debut in the Senior PGA Championship.

1981

- A new 30,000-square-foot PGA of America National Headquarters building is dedicated at PGA National Golf Course in Palm Beach Gardens, Florida.

1982

- Raymond Floyd wins his second PGA Championship and sets the tournament record of 132 for 36 holes; 200 for 54 holes; and ties the 18-hole record of 63.
- Don January wins his second Senior PGA Championship on the Champion Course at the new PGA National Golf Club in Palm Beach Gardens, Florida.
- Operation of the PGA World Golf Hall of Fame in Pinehurst, North Carolina, is transferred to the PGA of America.

1983

- The PGA National Golf Club, in Palm Beach Gardens, Florida, hosts the Ryder Cup. Captained by Jack Nicklaus, the United States edges Great Britain, 14 1/2–13 1/2.

1984

- The PGA of America, along with Oldsmobile, launches what is to become the most popular and largest pro-am golf tournament in the world, the Oldsmobile Scramble.
- Arnold Palmer wins his second Senior PGA Championship and ties a single-round tournament record with a 9-under-par 63.
- A contract is signed with Landmark Land Company to create PGA West in La Quinta, California.

1985

- Gary Player wins his second PGA Championship.
- Mississippi State University becomes the second college to offer the PGA Golf Management curriculum.
- The United States loses the Ryder Cup to Europe for first time since 1957, at the Belfry, Sutton Coldfield, England.

1986

- Membership in the PGA of America reaches 9,417, with an additional 5,111 apprentices.
- The PGA Scholarship Fund is established for children and grandchildren of PGA members.

1987

- Europe captures the Ryder Cup for the first time on American soil at Muirfield Village Golf Club, in Dublin, Ohio.
- The PGA National Golf Club in Palm Beach Gardens, Florida, hosts the PGA Championship.
- Jim Awtrey is named acting executive director, then is confirmed as executive director.

1988

- Jim Awtrey is named the PGA's first chief executive officer.
- New Mexico State University in Las Cruces becomes third school to offer the PGA Golf Management curriculum.

1989

- The Ben Hogan Tour started as part of a joint program between the PGA Tour and several PGA Sections.
- ESPN produces the first live cable coverage of the Senior PGA Championship.

1990

- The first live network coverage of Senior PGA Championship is broadcast on NBC Sports.
- The PGA grants NBC Sports and USA Network broadcast and cable rights to the 1991 and 1993 Ryder Cup.

1991

- Jack Nicklaus wins his first Seniors PGA Championship, at PGA National Golf Club, Palm Beach Gardens, Florida.
- Rookie John Daly, a last-minute addition and ninth alternate, stuns the golf world by capturing the 73rd PGA Championship at Crooked Stick Golf Club in Carmel, Indiana.

- Europe's Bernhard Langer misses a six-foot par putt on the 18th hole, allowing the United States to win the 29th Ryder Cup, 14 1/2–13 1/2, at the Ocean Course in Kiawah Island, South Carolina. It was the Americans' first Ryder Cup victory since 1983.
- The PGA Grand Slam of Golf is restructured to feature $1 million in prize money and more than eight hours of prime-time coverage on the Turner Sports network, reaching 57 million homes in the United States.
- Penn State University becomes the fourth school to offer a PGA Golf Management curriculum.
- The PGA of America celebrates its 75th anniversary with 19,932 members and 41 Sections.

1992

- The PGA of America enters the video market, announcing PGA Home Video at the 39th PGA Merchandise Show.
- Nick Price becomes eighth foreign-born PGA Champion at Bellerive Country Club, in St. Louis.
- The PGA Speed of Play Research Report is unveiled at Golf Summit '92 in Orlando, Florida, kicking off a nationwide campaign to improve the playing habits of the nation's more than 25 million amateur players.
- Membership in the PGA of America reaches 22,464, including 9,232 apprentices.

1993

- Tom Wargo, a PGA club professional from Centralia, Illinois, defeats Bruce Crampton in a 2-hole sudden-death playoff to win the Senior PGA Championship at PGA National Golf Club in Palm Beach Gardens, Florida.
- The PGA reaches more than 2,500 juniors through the PGA Kids on Course program with the National Association of Police Athletic/Activities Leagues and the NCAA's National Youth Sports Program.

- The PGA World Golf Hall of Fame in Pinehurst, North Carolina, merges with the new World Golf Village and its new international golf museum and Hall of Fame. The facility plans a 1995 opening near St. Augustine, Florida.
- Paul Azinger wins the 75th PGA Championship, defeating Greg Norman in a 2-hole sudden-death playoff at Inverness Club in Toledo, Ohio.
- Led by singles victories by Chip Beck, Davis Love III, and 51-year-old Raymond Floyd, the United States defeats Europe, 15–13, in the 30th Ryder Cup, at the Belfry in Sutton Coldfield, England.

1994

- Ernie Sabayrac, who revolutionized PGA Professional merchandising, becomes the namesake and first recipient of the Ernie Sabayrac Award for Lifetime Contributions to the Golf Industry.
- Arnold Palmer, competing in his 37th and final PGA Championship, receives the PGA's Distinguished Service Award at Southern Hills Country Club in Tulsa, Oklahoma.
- Nick Price, a winner of the British Open a month earlier, cruises to a PGA Championship-record 269 (11-under-par) for 72 holes at Southern Hills Country Club in Tulsa, Oklahoma.
- A record qualifying field of more than 11,000 youngsters nationwide participates in the Junior PGA Championship.
- The Golf Professional Training Program (GPTP), the PGA of America's first major renovation of the PGA's Education Program since 1970, debuts at the first of many training sites in Irvine, California.

1995

- Raymond Floyd, who suffered a final-round collapse a year earlier at PGA National Golf Club, takes command in the third round and wins the 56th Senior PGA Championship in Palm Beach Gardens, Florida.

- Patty Berg, cofounder of the Ladies Professional Golf Association, receives the PGA's Distinguished Service Award at Riviera Country Club in Pacific Palisades, California.
- Australian Steve Elkington rallies from a 6-stroke deficit, winning a 1-hole playoff with Scotland's Colin Montgomerie at the 77th PGA Championship at Riviera Country Club.
- The PGA announces the creation of PGA CareerLinks, an employment identification system linking employer requirements with the skills of PGA Professionals.
- Europe stages a dramatic final-day rally to defeat the United States, 14 1/2–13 1/2, in the 31st Ryder Cup at Oak Hill Country Club in Rochester, New York.

1996

- The 43rd PGA Merchandise Show, in its grandest scale ever, attracts 43,805 attendees from more than 70 countries, and more than 1,130 exhibitors to Orlando, Florida.
- Hale Irwin wins the 57th Senior PGA Championship in his first attempt.
- The PGA unveils the PGA Junior Series, a summer golf program for boys and girls ages 13 to 17. The initial series schedule touches 10 states and 10 PGA Sections.
- Mark Brooks of Fort Worth, Texas, defeats Kentuckian Kenny Perry in a 1-hole playoff in the PGA Championship at Valhalla Golf Club in Louisville.
- The United States draws with Great Britain and Ireland, 13–13, in the 18th PGA Cup in Perthshire, Scotland.
- Tiger Woods, a 20-year-old sensation who captures two earlier PGA Tour events, is elected to PGA of America membership and ranks 14th in the final 1996 U.S. Ryder Cup team standings.
- The PGA Golf Club, the first owned and operated public golf course by the PGA of America, debuts in Port St. Lucie, Florida.

- Hale Irwin posts a final-round 68, for a 12-stroke victory, and his second-consecutive Senior PGA Championship. Irwin becomes the first back-to-back repeat winner since Sam Snead in 1972–73.
- Bruce Zabriski of Rye, New York, wins the 30th PGA Club Professional Championship at Pinehurst Resort and Country Club in North Carolina. The CPC is the first to be televised nationally on the Golf Channel to its nearly 20 million viewers.
- With a rainbow breaking overhead as he steps to the 18th green, Davis Love III birdies the 72nd hole with an 11-under-par 269 total to win the 79th PGA Championship at Winged Foot Golf Club in Mamaroneck, New York.
- Tiger Woods, backed by his record-setting Masters victory in April and the season money title, wins the PGA Player of the Year Award in his first complete season on the PGA Tour.
- Guided by Captain Seve Ballesteros and some remarkable individual performances, Europe duplicates its 1-point victory in 1995 and defeats the United States, 14 1/2–13 1/2, in the 32nd Ryder Cup at Valderrama Golf Club in Sotogrande, Spain. It was the first Ryder Cup competition in continental Europe.

1998

- Hale Irwin becomes the first golfer since Eddie Williams (1942, 1945, 1946) to win three consecutive Senior PGA Championships.
- PGA Golf Club in Port St. Lucie, Florida, takes over as host of the Minority College Golf Championship.
- Vijay Singh, of Fiji, wins the 80th PGA Championship at Sahalee Country Club in Sammamish, Washington.
- The PGA Golf Club at PGA Village, in Port St. Lucie, Florida, expands by beginning construction of a third golf course, one designed by Pete Dye, and a prototype PGA Learning Center.

- Alice Dye, of Delray Beach, Florida, wife of the legendary golf course architect, becomes the first woman to join the PGA Board of Directors.
- The PGA Merchandise Show and the PGA International Golf Show, the world's largest golf expositions, are purchased by Reed Exhibition Companies of Norwalk, Connecticut, one of the world's largest trade show companies. The PGA retains an interest in both shows, while Reed produces and manages both expositions.
- The PGA of America, along with the PGA Tour, creates the Ryder Cup Outreach Program, which will allocate an estimated $13 million from the Ryder Cup for game outreach and an endowment for PGA Professional education.

1999

- Gene Sarazen, the longest-serving PGA member and winner of golf's Grand Slam, dies on May 13, at the age of 97. Sarazen was elected to PGA membership on March 15, 1921.
- Tiger Woods, 23, becomes the fifth-youngest winner ever when he captures the 81st PGA Championship, at the Medinah Country Club in Illinois.
- The United States, capped by Justin Leonard's 45-foot birdie putt on the 17th hole, stages the biggest comeback in Ryder Cup history to defeat Europe 14 1/2– 13 1/2 at The Country Club in Brookline, Mass.
- Payne Stewart, the 1989 PGA Champion, dies in a jet accident in Mina, South Dakota.
- The PGA announces that it will conduct the Senior PGA Championship outside of Florida for the first time since 1938, when it stages the 2001 Championship at Ridgewood Country Club in Paramus, New Jersey.
- The Dye Course, the third 18-hole course at PGA Golf Club in Port St. Lucie, Florida, opens to the public.

2000

- Jack Nicklaus is named recipient of PGA Distinguished Service Award.
- Doug Tewell captures a rain-hampered Senior PGA Championship by 7 strokes, with a 15-under-par 201 total at PGA National Golf Club, in Palm Beach Gardens, Florida.
- Tim Thelen of Richmond, Texas, defeats Mark Brown of Glen Cove, New York, in the first 5-hole cumulative score playoff in the 33rd PGA Club Professional Championship. Lightning canceled the final round, but skies cleared long enough to allow the playoff at Oak Tree Golf Club in Edmond, Oklahoma.
- Tiger Woods defeats Bob May in a first-ever 3-hole cumulative score playoff at Valhalla Golf Club, in Louisville, and becomes the first player in the stroke-play era to win back-to-back PGA Championships.

2001

- Tom Watson edges Jim Thorpe by 1 stroke to win the renamed Senior PGA Championship at the Ridgewood Country Club in Paramus, New Jersey.
- Wayne DeFrancesco of Baltimore, Maryland, a survivor of three back operations, goes wire-to-wire to win the 34th PGA Club Professional Championship at Crosswater Club in Sunriver, Oregon.
- Korean-born Inbee Park of Eustis, Florida, 13, wins the girls' division of the Junior PGA Championship.
- Ten players from the United States and Europe are selected to meet in the first Junior Ryder Cup at the K Club in Straffan, near Dublin, Ireland. The competition is the first formal connection between the PGA and Ryder Cup Ltd.
- Sparked by a third-round hole-in-one, David Toms wins the 83rd PGA Championship at Atlanta Athletic Club with a record 72-hole total of 265.

- The PGA of America's 41 Sections nationwide contribute to the American Red Cross Disaster Fund for the families of victims of the September 11 terrorist attacks, contributing $500,000 to match the donations of U.S. Ryder Cup Team members toward the Relief Fund.
- Calling it the "best in what modern education and training can offer," the PGA of America President Jack Connelly dedicates the PGA Education Center, November 8, at PGA Village in Port. St. Lucie, Florida.

2002

- Fuzzy Zoeller scores his first victory in 15 years, 10 months, and 27 days, by winning the 63rd Senior PGA Championship at Firestone Country Club in Akron, Ohio.
- Barry Evans of Charleston, West Virginia., wins the 35th PGA Club Professional Championship at Valhalla Golf Club in Louisville, Kentucky. Suzy Whaley, of Farmington, Connecticut, becomes the first woman Professional to compete in the Championship, and misses the 36-hole cut by 5 strokes.
- Rich Beem of El Paso, Texas, a former cellular telephone salesman, son of a PGA Professional and a former PGA Assistant Professional, holds off Tiger Woods to win the 84th PGA Championship.
- Suzy Whaley, a PGA head professional at Blue Fox Run Golf Club in Avon, Connecticut, becomes the first woman to win a PGA Section Championship by capturing the Connecticut PGA title. With her victory, Whaley earned a berth in the 2003 Greater Hartford Open, making her the first woman since Babe Zaharias in 1945 to qualify for a PGA Tour event.
- Delayed one year after the terrorist attacks upon America, the 34th Ryder Cup resumes at the Belfry in Sutton Coldfield, England. Europe breaks an 8–8 deadlock by dominating the final-day singles for a 15–12 victory.
- The PGA Museum of Golf is dedicated on December 4, at PGA Village in Port St. Lucie, Florida.

2003

- PGA Professional Tim Thelen, of Richmond, Texas, wins his second PGA Professional National Championship.
- PGA club professional Suzy Whaley, of Farmington, Connecticut, posts rounds of 75 and 78 on July 24 and 25, before missing the cut in the Greater Hartford Open.
- Winless in 163 previous starts on the PGA Tour, unheralded Shaun Micheel posts a 2-stroke victory over Chad Campbell in the 85th PGA Championship at Oak Hill Country Club.

2004

- The PGA of America leads in the launch of "Play Golf America," an industry-supported growth of the game initiative aimed at attracting new golfers and bringing back former or occasional golfers through a variety of programs to be guided by PGA Professionals.
- Vijay Singh captures his second PGA Championship, defeating Chris DiMarco and Justin Leonard in a 3-hole aggregate score playoff at Whistling Straits near Kohler, Wisconsin.
- Bernhard Langer captains Europe to a dominating 18 1/2–9 1/2 victory over the United States in the 35th Ryder Cup at Oakland Hills Country Club in Bloomfield Hills, Michigan.
- Hale Irwin survives five weather-related delays, tornado warnings, and more than seven inches of rain to beat Jay Haas by 1 stroke at the 65th Senior PGA Championship at Valhalla Golf Club, in Louisville, Kentucky. Irwin, one week shy of his 59th birthday, earns his fourth Senior PGA title.
- Masters Champion Phil Mickelson fires a 59 to win the 22nd PGA Grand Slam of Golf at Poipu Bay in Kauai, Hawaii.

2005

- Mike Reid eagles the 72nd hole to force a three-way playoff, then birdies the first playoff hole to defeat Dana Quigley and Jerry Pate in the 66th Senior PGA Championship at Laurel Valley Golf Club in Ligonier, Pennsylvania.
- Phil Mickelson returned on a Monday at Baltusrol Golf Club to become the first left-hander to win a PGA Championship and the first left-hander to win more than one major.
- The PGA Hall of Fame is unveiled at the PGA Museum of Golf in Port St. Lucie, Florida, featuring 122 inductees that have made significant contributions to the Association since its origin in 1916.
- The PGA of America teams with major U.S. golf organizations to raise more than $1.3 million for the U.S. Golf Hurricane Katrina Relief Fund, to provide support for relief efforts in devastated areas of the Gulf Coast.
- Joe Steranka, who guided the PGA of America's communications and broadcasting divisions, is named to succeed Jim Awtrey as chief executive officer.
- The PGA Grand Slam of Golf is won by Tiger Woods for a record sixth time.
- Tiger Woods wins a record seventh PGA Player of the Year Award and a record sixth Vardon Trophy.

2006

- The PGA of America holds a 90th Anniversary gala event on April 10, 2006, at the former Hotel Martinique (now the Radisson Martinique), in New York City, the site of its founding in 1916.
- Jay Haas defeats Brad Bryant in a 3-hole playoff at Oak Tree Golf Club in Edmond, Oklahoma, to win the 67th Senior PGA Championship.
- Ron Philo Jr. of Westchester, New York, defeats Alan Schulte of Fishers, Indiana, on the third extra hole to capture the 39th PGA Professional National Championship at Turning Stone Casino and Resort in Verona, New York.

- Tiger Woods finished a 5-stroke triumph in the 88th PGA Championship at Medinah Country Club in Illinois and became the first person to win the PGA Championship twice at the same venue.
- Led by Darren Clarke and Colin Montgomerie, Europe routs the United States in the 36th Ryder Cup at the K Club, 18 1/2–9 1/2.
- Paul Azinger is named the 25th United States Ryder Cup Captain and works with the PGA of America officials to launch a new points system to determine the U.S. Team for the 37th Ryder Cup in 2008.

2007
- Erasing a 24-year winless streak, South African Denis Watson captures the 68th Senior PGA Championship, May 27, at the Ocean Course at Kiawah Island Golf Resort in South Carolina.
- Chip Sullivan of Troutville, Virginia, wins the 40th PGA Professional National Championship, June 24, at Crosswater Club at Sunriver, Oregon.
- Lexi Thompson, 12, of Coral Springs, Florida, becomes the youngest all-division winner in Junior PGA Championship history; while Chris DeForest of Cottekill, New York, wins the boys' title.
- Tiger Woods overcomes a world-class field and a week of 100-plus-degree weather at Southern Hills Country Club in Tulsa, Oklahoma, to win the 89th PGA Championship, for his fourth PGA Championship.
- Inspired by Captain Dan Rooney, a PGA Professional and F-16 fighter pilot from Broken Arrow, Oklahoma, Patriot Golf Day is launched on September 1, at golf facilities nationwide. More than 3,200 facilities combine to donate more than $1.1 million in scholarship support for the families of veterans who were injured or perished.

2008
- Jay Haas captures his second Senior PGA Championship title, contested at Oak Hill Country Club in Rochester, New York
- Scott Hebert, of Traverse City, Michigan, rallies from a 3-stroke deficit with birdies on five of his first seven holes of the back nine to capture the 41st PGA Professional National Championship by 1 stroke, June 22, at Reynolds Plantation in Greensboro, Georgia.
- Ireland's Pádraig Harrington captures the 90th PGA Championship at Oakland Hills for his third major championship and his second PGA title.
- The United States snaps a nine-year victory drought and topples Europe, 16 1/2–11 1/2, in the 37th Ryder Cup at Valhalla Golf Club.

2009
- Get Golf Ready, Play Golf America's featured program for 2009, is launched at the PGA Merchandise Show in Orlando, Florida.
- Michael Allen, in his first Champions Tour outing, wins the 70th Senior PGA Championship in May at Canterbury Golf Club outside of Cleveland.
- PGA Life Member William (Bill) Powell of East Canton, Ohio, the only African-American to build, own, and operate a golf course in the United States, receives the PGA Distinguished Service Award.
- Korea's Y. E. Yang defeats Tiger Woods in the final round of the 91st PGA Championship at Hazeltine National Golf Club, becoming the first Asian male player ever to win a major.
- On October 9, the International Olympic Committee (IOC) votes to return golf to the Olympics in 2016 after an absence of more than a century.
- Sue Fiscoe of Modesto, California, is sworn in as the first woman director on the PGA Board. Independent Director Asuka Nakahara of Merion, Pennsylvania, becomes the first Asian-American to gain a berth on that body.

- At an emotion-filled 94th PGA Annual Meeting in New Orleans, the PGA bestows posthumous membership upon African-American golf pioneers John Shippen, Bill Spiller, and Ted Rhodes; and designates posthumous honorary membership to boxing legend turned diversity-in-golf advocate Joe Louis Barrow.

2010

- Former U.S. Ryder Cup Captain Tom Lehman defeats Fred Couples and David Frost in a 1-hole playoff to capture the 71st Senior PGA Championship at Colorado Golf Club in Parker, Colorado.
- University of Illinois Coach Mike Small wins a record-tying third PGA Professional National Championship at French Lick Resort in Indiana.
- Germany's Martin Kaymer defeats American Bubba Watson in a 3-hole playoff at Whistling Straits in Kohler, Wisconsin, becoming the first from his homeland and the third straight non-American to win a PGA Championship.
- With rain forcing the first Monday conclusion in event history, Europe holds off a charge by the United States in singles to win the 37th Ryder Cup, 14 1/2–13 1/2.
- Suzy Whaley joins Sue Fiscoe on the national board of the PGA.

2011

- Tom Watson birdies the 18th hole at Valhalla Golf Club, defeating David Eger in a 2-hole playoff and capturing the 73rd Senior PGA Championship presented by KitchenAid.
- David Hutsell of Baltimore, Maryland, takes the 44th PGA Professional National Championship at Hershey Country Club in Pennsylvania, winning a three-player, 2-hole playoff.
- Competing in his first major championship, Keegan Bradley of Jupiter, Florida, stuns the golf world by defeating Jason Dufner in a 3-hole aggregate score playoff to capture the 93rd PGA Championship at Atlanta Athletic Club.

- The United States wins six of eight foursome matches on the way to a 17 1/2–8 1/2 victory over Great Britain and Ireland in the 25th PGA Cup at CordeValle in San Martin, California.
- PGA apprentice professional Chad Pfeifer, 30, of Scottsdale, Arizona, a veteran who lost a leg during service in Iraq, wins the inaugural Warrior Open hosted by former President George W. Bush in Irving, Texas.
- Samuel Henry "Errie" Ball, the last surviving member of the 1934 Masters field, and PGA Honorary President Jim Remy, heads seven inductees into the PGA Golf Professional Hall of Fame.

2012

- Roger Chapman of England cruises to a wire-to-wire triumph in the 74th Senior PGA Championship presented by KitchenAid at Harbor Shores in Benton Harbor, Michigan, becoming the first Englishman and the first European since Jock Hutchison in 1947 to hoist the Alfred S. Bourne Trophy.
- Jason Montoya of Santa Ana Pueblo, New Mexico, is the first Native American to be elected to PGA membership.
- Matt Dobyns of Sea Cliff, New York, completes a record-breaking 8-stroke triumph to shatter Sam Snead's 41-year victory margin record and win the 45th PGA Professional National Championship at Bayonet and Black Horse in Seaside, California.
- Northern Ireland's Rory McIlroy completes a historic performance on the Ocean Course at Kiawah Island Golf Resort in South Carolina, taking the PGA Championship by a record 8 strokes. He breaks Jack Nicklaus's victory margin standard by 1 stroke.
- Sparked by England's Ian Poulter, Europe rallies from a 4-point deficit in the Sunday singles at Medinah Country Club in Illinois to stun the United States and retain the Ryder Cup by a 14 1/2–13 1/2 margin.

- Peter Bevacqua, a native of Bedford, New York, is named to succeed Joe Steranka as the third chief executive officer in PGA of America history.
- Black pioneers William Powell and Jimmie DeVoe and PGA Honorary President Allen Wronowski head eight inductees into the PGA of America Hall of Fame. The inductees include Bob Toski, Michael Hebron, Bill Ogden, Jim Mrva, and Don "Chip" Essig IV.

2013

- PGA Teaching Professional Susie Meyers becomes the first woman PGA member to coach PGA Tour players to victory, with students Michael Thompson winning the Honda Classic and Derek Ernst the Wells Fargo Championship.
- Japan's Kohki Idoki, closing with a near-flawless 65 at Bellerive Country Club near St. Louis, prevails in the Senior PGA Championship presented by KitchenAid. The victory came on Idoki's first-ever visit to America.
- Jason Dufner closes with a 68 for a 2-stroke victory over Jim Furyk and wins the PGA Championship at Oak Hill Country Club near Rochester, New York.

2014

- KPMG, the PGA of America, and the LPGA announce the new KPMG Women's PGA Championship and the creation of a multifaceted program focused on the advancement and empowerment of women on and off the golf course.
- Scotland's Colin Montgomerie closes with a 65 to defeat Tom Watson by 4 strokes and win the Senior PGA Championship presented by KitchenAid at Harbor Shores in Benton Harbor, Michigan.
- PGA Hall of Famer Errie Ball passes at age 103, having served a PGA record 83 years.
- President Bill Clinton receives the PGA Distinguished Service Award in Louisville.

- Rory McIlroy rallies just before sunset to defeat Phil Mickelson by 1 stroke and capture his second PGA Championship in three years, at Valhalla Golf Club in Louisville, Kentucky.
- Europe added another chapter of Ryder Cup dominance, this time at Gleneagles in Scotland, posting a 16 1/2 to 11 1/2 victory over the United States.
- Derek Sprague of Malone, New York, is elected the 39th president of the PGA of America, while Suzy Whaley of Farmington, Connecticut, is elected Secretary becoming the first woman to serve as a national officer in PGA history.

2015

- Scotland's Colin Montgomerie wins a second consecutive Senior PGA Championship presented by KitchenAid at French Lick Resort in Indiana.
- South Korea's Inbee Park matches Annika Sörenstam by winning a third consecutive KPMG Women's PGA Championship (formerly LPGA Championship) at Westchester Country Club in Rye, New York.
- Matt Dobyns of Glen Head, New York, captures a second PGA Professional National Championship by 1 stroke at the Philadelphia Cricket Club.
- Australian Jason Day sets a major championship record 20-under-par for 72 holes to capture the 97th PGA Championship at Whistling Straits near Kohler, Wisconsin.

2016

- The PGA of America, with some 28,000 men and women member professionals. celebrates its centennial on April 10.
- The 98th PGA Championship marks a return to Baltusrol Golf Club.
- After a 112-year absence, golf returns to the Olympic Games in Rio de Janeiro, Brazil.
- The 41st Ryder Cup is conducted at Hazeltine National Golf Club in Chaska, Minnesota.

	NAME	SECTION	TERM OF OFFICE
1st	Robert White	Metropolitan	1916-1919
2nd	Jack Mackie	Metropolitan	1919-1920
3rd	George Sargent	Southeastern	1921-1926
4th	Alex Pirie	Metropolitan	1927-1930
5th	Charles Hall	Southeastern	1931-1932
6th	George Jacobus	New Jersey	1933-1939
7th	Tom Walsh	Illinois	1940-1941
8th	Ed Dudley	Colorado	1942-1948
9th	Joe Novak	Southern California	1949-1951
10th	Horton Smith	Michigan	1952-1954
11th	Harry Moffitt	Northern Ohio	1955-1957
12th	Harold Sargent	Southeastern	1958-1960
13th	Lou Strong	Illinois	1961-1963
14th	Warren Cantrell	Texas	1964-1965
15th	Max Elbin	Middle Atlantic	1966-1968
16th	Leo Fraser	Philadelphia	1969-1970
17th	Warren Orlick	Michigan	1971-1972
18th	William Clarke	Middle Atlantic	1973-1974
19th	Henry Poe	Dixie	1975-1976
20th	Don Padgett	Indiana	1977-1978
21st	Frank Cardi	Metropolitan	1979-1980
22nd	Joe Black	Northern Texas	1981-1982
23rd	Mark Kizziar	South Central	1983-1984
24th	Mickey Powell	Indiana	1985-1986
25th	James Ray Carpenter	Gulf States	1987-1988
26th	Patrick J. Rielly	Southern California	1989-1990
27th	Dick Smith	Philadelphia	1991-1992
28th	Gary Schaal	Carolinas	1993-1994
29th	Tom Addis III	Southern California	1995-1996
30th	Ken Lindsay	Gulf States	1997-1998
31st	Will Mann	Carolinas	1999-2000
32nd	Jack Connelly	Philadelphia	2001-2002
33rd	M.G. Orender	North Florida	2003-2004
34th	Roger Warren	Carolinas	2005-2006
35th	Brian Whitcomb	Southwest	2007-2008
36th	Jim Remy	New England	2009-2010
37th	Allen Wronowski	Middle Atlantic	2011-2012
38th	Ted Bishop	Indiana	2013-2014
39th	Derek Sprague	Northeastern New York	2015-2016

BIBLIOGRAPHY

Books

A

Acree, Edward C., with Hutchison, Jock and Bill, *Golf Simplified:* Ziff-Davis Publishing Chicago 1946

Acushnet Company, *The Script: Celebration of a Timeless Brand: 75 Years and Still Counting:* Acushnet Company Fairhaven, Massachusetts 2010

Adams, John, *The Parks of Musselburgh: Golfers, Architects, Clubmakers:* Grant Books, Worcestershire 1991

Adamson, Alistair Beaton, *Allan Robertson: His Life and Times:* Grant Books, Worcestershire, Scotland 1985

Auwater, Raymond G., *Nassau Country Club: The Place To Be 1896-1996:* Nassau Country Club Glen Cove 1996

B

Bahto, George, *The Evangelist of Golf: The Story of Charles Blair Macdonald:* Clock Tower Press Chelsea, Michigan 2002

Barclay, James A., *Golf in Canada: A History:* McClelland & Steward Inc. Toronto, 1992

Barkow, Al with Sarazen, Mary Ann, *Gene Sarazen and Shell's Wonderful World of Golf:* Clock Tower Press Ann Arbor 2003

Barkow, Al, *Getting' to the Dance Floor: An Oral History of American Golf:* Atheneum New York 1986

Barkow, Al, *The Golden Era of Golf: How America Rose to Dominate the Old Scot Game:* Thomas Dunne Books New York 2000

Barkow, Al, *Golf's Golden Grind: The History of the PGA Tour:* Harcourt, Brace, Jovanovich New York 1974

Barnes, James M., *A Guide to Good Golf:* London John Lane The Bodley Head LTD. 1925

Barnes, James M., *Picture Analysis of Golf Strokes: A Complete Book of Instruction:* J.B. Lippincott Company Philadelphia 1919

Bendelow, Stuart W., *Thomas 'Tom' Bendelow: The Johnny Appleseed of American Golf:* Williams & Company Savannah 2006

Behrend, John, and Lewis, Peter N., *Challenges and Champions: The Royal & Ancient Golf Club 1754-1883 Volume 1:* Grant Books Worcestershire 1998

Behrend, John, Lewis, Peter N. and Mackie, Keith, *Champions & Guardians: The Royal & Ancient Golf Club 1884-1939 Volume 2:* Grant Books Worcestershire 2001

Bloomfield, Gary L., *Duty, Honor, Victory: America's Athletes in World War II:* The Lyons Press, Guilford, Connecticut 2004

Bohn, Michael K., *Money Golf: 600 Years of Bettin' on Birdies:* Potomac Books Washington D.C. 2007

Boston Globe, *Golfing New England: Courses, Legends, History, and Hints:* Triumph Books Chicago 2007

Braid, James, *Advanced Golf: Or, Hints And Instruction For Progressive Players:* George W. Jacobs & Company Philadelphia 1908

Brenner, Morgan G., *The Majors of Golf: Complete Results of The Open, the U.S. Open, the PGA Championship, and the Masters, 1860-2008 3 Volume Set:* McFarland & Company Jefferson, North Carolina 2009

Browning, Robert, *A History of Golf: The Royal & Ancient Game:* J.M. Dent & Sons Ltd, London 1955

Bryan, James, *Seven Ages of Golfing Genius:* Author House UK Limited Central Milton Keynes, England 2009

Burgess, Charles D., *Golf Links: Chay Burgess, Francis Ouimet, and The Bringing of Golf to America:* Rounder Books Cambridge, Massachusetts 2005

Burke, Jr., Jackie, with Yocom, Guy, *It's Only A Game: Words of Wisdom from a Lifetime in Golf:* Gotham Books New York 2006

Byrdy, Stan, *Augusta and Aiken In Golf's Golden Age:* Arcadia Publishing Charleston 2002

Campbell, Malcolm, *The Scottish Golf Book:* Sports Publishing Champaign, Illinois 2002

C

Carlisle, Robert D.B., *The Montclair Golf Club: A Way of Life 1893-1983:* Kingsport Press Tennessee 1984

Carlsen, Spike, *The Splintered History of Wood: Belt Sander Races, Blind Woodworkers & Baseball Bats:* Collins New York 2008

Chambers, Robert, *A Few Rambling Remarks on Golf with The Rules As Laid Down By The Royal & Ancient Club of St Andrews:* W. & R. Chambers London & Edinburgh 1862 USGA Facsimile 1983

Chapman, Kenneth G., *The Rules of the Green: A History of the Rules of Golf:* Triumph Books Chicago 1997

Christian, Frank, with Brown, Cal, *Augusta National & The Masters: A Photographers Scrapbook:* Sleeping Bear Press Chelsea, Michigan 1996

Clark, Robert, *Golf: A Royal and Ancient Game:* Privately published by R. and R. Clark Edinburgh 1875

Clavin, Tom, *Sir Walter: Walter Hagen and the Invention of Professional Golf:* Simon & Schuster New York 2005

Colville, George M., *5 Open Champions and The Musselburgh Golf Story:* Colville Books Musselburgh, East Lothian 1980

Companiotte, John, *Jimmy Demaret: The Swing's the Thing:* Clock Tower Press Ann Arbor 2004

Concannon, Dale, *Bullets, Bombs, & Birdies: Golf In the Time of War:* Clock Tower Press Ann Arbor, 2003

Concannon, Dale, *Golf The Early Days: Royal & Ancient Game From Its Origins to 1939:* Smithmark Publishers New York 1995

Cook, Kevin, *Tommy's Honor: The Story of Old Tom Morris and Young Tom Morris, Golf's Founding Father and Son:* Gotham Books New York 2007

Cornish, Geoffrey S. and Whitten, Ronald E., *The Golf Course:* Rutledge Press New York 1981

Cousins, Geoffrey, *Golfers At Law:* Stanley Paul & Company London 1958

Cousins, Geoffrey, *Lords of the Links: The Story of Professional Golf:* Hutchinson Benham, London, England 1977

Cronin, Tim, *A Century of Golf: Western Golf Association 1899-1999:* Sleeping Bear Press Chelsea, Michigan 1998

Cronin, Tim, *The Spirit of Medinah: 75 Years of Fellowship and Championships:* Medinah Country Club Medinah, Illinois 2001

Crosset, Todd W., *Outsiders in the Clubhouse: The World of Women's Professional Golf:* State University of New York Press Albany 1995

D

Darwin, Bernard, *British Golf:* Collins London 1946

Darwin, Bernard, *Golf Between Two Wars:* Chatto & Windus London 1944

Darwin, Bernard, *Golf from the Times:* The Times London 1912

Darwin, Bernard, *The Golf Courses of the British Isles:* Duckworth & Co London 2010

Davies, Peter, *Davies' Dictionary of Golfing Terms:* Simon & Schuster New York 1980

Dawkins, Marvin P. and Kinloch, Graham C. Kinloch, *African American Golfers During the Jim Crow Era:* Praeger Westport, Connecticut 2000

De la Torre, Manuel, *Understanding The Golf Swing:* Skyhorse Publishing New York 2008

De Grout, Colin, with Webster, Jim, *Pro Golf: Out of the Rough: Illustrated history of professional golf in Australia:* Professional Golfers' Association of Australia Cattai 1991

De St. Jorre, John, *The Story of Golf at The Country Club:* Hasak Wellington, Florida 2009

Dedman, Robert H. with DeLoach, Debbie, *King of Clubs: Grow Rich in More Than Money:* Taylor Publishing Dallas 1999

Demaret, Jimmy, *My Partner Ben Hogan:* McGraw-Hill New York 1954

Dennis, Larry with photos by Machat, Udo, *The Golf Ball Book:* Sport Images Oakland 2000

Diperna, Paula and Keller, Vikki, *Oakhurst: The Birth and Rebirth of America's First Golf Course:* Walker & Company New York 2002

Dobereiner, Peter, *The Glorious World of Golf:* A Ridge Press Book New York 1984

Dodd, Hugh, and Purdie, Professor David, *The Greatest Game: The Ancyent & Healthfulle Exercyse of the Golff:* MacLean Dubois Edinburgh 2010

Dodson, James, *A Golfer's Life: Arnold Palmer:* Ballantine Books New York 1999

Dodson, James, *American Triumvirate: Sam Snead, Byron Nelson, Ben Hogan, and the Modern Age of Golf:* Alfred A. Knopf New York 2012

Dodson, James, *Ben Hogan: An American Life:* Doubleday New York 2004

Duino, Louis, *San Jose Golf and Country Club: 75th Anniversary 1912-1987:* San Jose Country Club San Jose 1987

Dunn, Bob and Mulvoy, Mark, *Apawamis: One Hundred Years of Excellence:* Sammis Publishing Norwalk, Connecticut 1990

Dunn, Seymour, *Golf Fundamentals:* Seymour Dunn Lake Placid 1922

Dye, Pete, with Shaw, Mike, *Bury Me in a Pot Bunker: New Special Edition:* Dye Shaw Books Superior, Colorado 2013

E

Elliott, Charles, *East Lake Country Club History: Home Course of Bobby Jones:* Cherokee Publishing Atlanta 1984

Elliott, Len and Kelly Barbara, *Who's Who In Golf:* Arlington House New Rochelle 1976

Ellis, Jeffery, *The Clubmakers' Art: Antique Golf Clubs and their History:* Zephyr Productions Oak Harbor, Washington 1997

Ellis, Ray, and Wright, Ben, *The Spirit of Golf:* Longstreet Press Marietta, Georgia 1992

Evans Jr., Charles *Chick Evans' Golf Book: The Story of the Sporting Battles of the Greatest of all Amateur Golfers:* Thos, E. Wilson & Co. by The Reilly & Lee Co. Chicago 1921

Eubanks, Steve, *To Win and Die in Dixie: The Birth of the Modern Golf Swing and the Mysterious Death of Its Creator:* Ballantine Books New York 2010

F

Farrell, Johnny, *If I Were In Your Golf Shoes:* Henry Holt & Company New York 1951

Fields, Bill, *Arnie, Seve, and a Fleck of Golf History: Heroes, Underdogs, Courses, and Championships:* University of Nebraska Press Lincoln 2014

Finegan, James W., *A Centennial Tribute to Golf In Philadelphia:* Golf Association of Philadelphia Philadelphia 1996

Finegan, James W., *Pine Vally Golf Club: A Unique Haven of the Game:* Pine Valley Golf Club New Jersey 2000

Finegan, James W., *Where Golf Is Great: The Finest Courses of Scotland and Ireland:* Artisan New York 2006

Flaherty, Tom, *The U.S. Open 1895-1965: The complete story of the United States Golf Championship:* E.P. Dutton & Co. New York 1966

Flannery, Michael and Leech, Richard, *Golf Through the Ages: Six Hundred Years of Golfing Art:* Golf Links Press Iowa 2004

Fountain, David E., *Grooves: How Jock Hutchison and His Grooved Clubs Changed Golf History!;* CyPress Publications Tallahassee, Florida 2010

Francis. Richard S., *Golf: Its Rules and Decisions:* The Macmillan Company New York 1937

Frost, David, *The Greatest Game Ever Played: Harry Vardon, Francis Ouimet, and the Birth of Modern Golf:* Hyperion Press New York 2002 (Advance Reading Copy)

Frost, Mark, *The Grand Slam: Bobby Jones, America, and the Story of Golf:* Hyperion New York 2004

G

Galbraith, William, *Prestwick St. Nicholas Golf Club:* Committee of Prestwick St. Nicholas Golf Club – Centenary of the Club, Prestwick, Scotland 1951

Geddes, Olive M., *A Swing Through Time: Golf In Scotland 1457-1744:* National Library of Scotland, Edinburgh, Scotland 2007

Georgiady, Peter, *The Compendium of British Club Makers:* Airlie Hall Press Kernersville, North Carolina 1994 (Third Edition 2004)

Georgiady, Peter, *North American Club Makers:* Airlie Hall Press Greensboro, North Carolina 1998

Gibson, William H., *Early Irish Golf: The First Courses, Clubs and Pioneers:* Oakleaf Publications Kildare 1988

Gilson, C.J.L., *Golf:* Frederick Warne & Co., LTD. London 1928

Gibson, Nevin H., *The Encyclopedia of Golf:* A.S. Barnes and Company New York 1958

Gionta, Elizabeth, *Colonial The Tournament: 60 Years of Greatness:* Panache Partners Dallas 2006

Glanville, Bob, *Golf: The Game of Lessening Failures:* Trafford Publishing Bloomington, Indiana 2011

Glenn, Rhonda, *The Illustrated History of Women's Golf:* Taylor Publishing Dallas 1991

Goodner, Ross, *Chicago Golf Club 1892-1992:* Chicago Golf Club Wheaton 1991

Goodwin, Stephen, *Bandon Dunes: Golf As It Was Meant to Be: Collector's Edition:* Skybox Press San Diego 2014

Goodwin, Stephen, *Dream Golf: The Making of Bandon Dunes:* Algonquin Books Chapel Hill 2006

Gould, David, *Q School Confidential:* Thomas Dunne Books New York 1999

Govedarica, Tom, *Chicago Golf: The First 100 Years:* Eagle Communications Group Chicago 1991

Graffis, Herb, *The PGA: The Official History of the Professional Golfers' Association of America;* Thomas Y. Crowell Company New York 1975

Graubart, Julian I., *Golf's Greatest Championship: The 1960 U.S. Open:* Donald I. Fine Books New York 1997

Guterbridge, David E., *The Biography of Marion Hollins: Champion in a Man's World:* Sleeping Bear Press Chelsea, Michigan 1998

H

Haas, Gene, *Playing Through 1901-2001: A History of the Wisconsin State Golf Association:* Wisconsin State Golf Association Brookfield 2001

Hackney, Stewart, *Carnoustie Links: Courses and Players:* Ravensbay Publications Dundee 1988

Hagen, John Peter, *'Play Away Please': The Tale of the Sale of Golf's Greates Icon – The St Andrews Old Course Starter's Box:* Mainstream Publishing Edinburgh 2010

Hagen, Walter, *The Walter Hagen Story: I never wanted to be a millionaire – I just wanted to live like one...* Simon & Schuster New York 1956

Hamilton, David, *Early Golf at St. Andrews:* The Patrick Press Glasgow 1986

Hamilton, David, *Golf: Scotland's Game:* The Patrick Press Kilmacolm Scotland 1998

Harmon, Claude "Butch" Harmon, Jr., with Steve Eubanks, *The Pro: Lessons About Golf and Life from My Father, Claude Harmon, Sr.:* Three Rivers Press New York 2006

Hartman, Robert, *Tales From Pinehurst; Stories From the Mecca of American Golf:* Sports Publishing Champaign, Illinois 2004

Hayes, John, *Learning Golf with Manuel:* Hayes Golf Pro Publishing St. Louis 2009

van Hengle, Stephen J.H., *Early Golf:* Frank P. Van Eck Publishers, Vadfuz, Liechtenstein 1985

Healy, Kay, *75 Years at Oakland Hills: A Jubilee Celebration:* Perry & White Warren, Michigan 1991

Henderson, Ian T. and Stirk, David I., *Golf in the Making:* Henderson & Stirk Ltd Near Winchester, Hants 1979

Hicks, Betty and Griffin, Ellen J., *Golf Manual For Teachers:* C.V. Mosby Company St. Louis 1949

Hicks, Betty, *My Life: From Fairway to Airway:* iUniverse New York 2006

Hogan, Ben with Wind, Herbert Warren, *Five Lessons: The Modern Fundamentals of Golf:* A.S. Barnes and Company New York 1957

Holanda, Ray, *The Golf of the Decade on the PGA Tour: From Walter Hagen in the 1920s to Tiger Woods in the 2000s:* iUniverse Bloomington, Indiana 2010

Holt, Richard, Lewis, Peter N., and Vamplew, Wray, *The Professional Golfers' Association 1901-2001: One hundred years of service to golf:* Grant Books, Worcestershire 2002

Hopkins, Jim, *Taylor's Gold: Life and times of a golfing superstar:* Edward Gaskell Publishers Devon, England 2010

Hosmer, Howard C., *From Little Acorns Volune II: The Story of Oak Hill 1901-1996:* Oak Hill Country Club Rochester, New York 1986

Hotelling, Neal, *Pebble Beach Golf Links: The Official History:* Sleeping Bear Press Chelsea, Michigan 1999

Howell, Audrey, *Harry Vardon: The Revealing Story of a Champion Golfer:* Stanley Paul & Co. London 1991

Hunter, Dave, *Golf Simplified: Cause & Effect:* Hodder and Stoughton London 1921

Hutchinson, Horace G., *Fifty Years of Golf:* United States Golf Association Facsimile of 1919 edition, Far Hills, New Jersey, 1985

Hutchinson, Horace G., *Golf: The Badminton Library:* Little, Brown, and Co. London 1890

J

Jarrett, Tom, and Mason, Peter, *St. Andrews Links: Six Centuries of Golf:* Mainstream Publishing Edinburgh 2009

Jenkins, Dan, *Jenkins at the Majors: Sixty Years of the World's Best Golf Writing, from Hogan to Tiger:* Doubleday New York 2009

Johns, Colonel Dick, *PGA Middle Atlantic Section: 2010 Annual:* Sheridan Books Ann Arbor 2009

Johnson, M. Mikell, *The African American Woman Golfer: Her Legacy:* Praeger West Port Connecticut 2008

Johnston, Alastair J. and James F., *The Chronicles of Golf: 1457 to 1857:* Alastair Johnson Cleveland 1993

Johnston, Alastair J., *The Clapcott Papers:* Privately Published Edinburgh 1985

Johnston, Alastair J., *Vardon to Woods: A Pictorial History of Golfers in Advertising:* Alastair Johnston Cleveland 1999

Jones, Ernest and Brown, Innis, *Swinging Into Golf:* Robert M. McBride & Company New York 1946

Joy, David, *St Andrews & The Open Championship: The Official History:* Sleeping Bear Press Chelsea, Michigan 1999

Joy, David, *The Scrapbook of Old Tom Morris:* Sleeping Bear Press Chelsea, Michigan 2001

K

Kahn, Liz, *The LPGA: The Unauthorized Version:* Group Fore Productions Menlo Park, California 1996

Kavanagh, L.V., *History of Golf in Canada:* Fitzhenry and Whiteside Limited Toronto 1973

Kennedy, John H., *A Course of Their Own: A History of African American Golfers:* Andrews McMeel Kansas City 2000

Kenny, Kevin, *American Golf in the Great Depression: The Pros Take to the Grapefruit Circuit:* McFarland & Company Jefferson, North Carolina 2014

Kerr, John, *The Golf Book of East Lothian (1896):* T. And A. Constable Edinburgh 1896

Kilpartick, Bill, *Brassies, Mashies, & Bootleg Scotch:* University of Nebraska Press Lincoln 2001

Kennington, Don, *The Source Book of Golf:* Oryx Press Phoenix 1981

Kirsch, George B., *Golf In America:* University of Illinois Press Urbana 2009

Kladstrup, Donald M., *The Crown Jewels of Oak Hill:* Oak Hill Country Club Rochester, New York 1989

Kroeger, Robert, *The Golf Courses of Old Tom Morris: A Look at Early Golf Course Architecture:* Heritage Communications, Cincinnati, Ohio 1995

L

Labbance, Bob, with Siplo, Brian, *The Vardon Invasion: Harry's Triumphant 1900 American Tour:* Sports Media Group Ann Arbor 2008

Labbance, Bob, Witteveen, Gordon, *Keepers of the Green: A History of Golf Course Management:* Ann Arbor Press and Golf Course Superintendents Association of America 2002

Labbance, Bob and White, Patrick, *The Country Club of Pittsfield: More Than A Century of History:* Notown Communications Montpelier, Vermont 2004

Labbance, Bob & Mendik, Kevin, *The Life and Work of Wayne Stiles:* Notown Communications Montpelier, Vermont 2008

Larrabee, Gary, *The Green & Golf Coast: The History of Golf on Boston's North Shore 1893-2001:* Commonwealth Editions Beverly, Massachusetts 2001

Latham, Richard A., *The Evolution of the Links at The Royal Country Down Golf Club:* Radial Sports Publishing Hertfordshire, Ireland 2006

Lee, James P., *Golf And Golfing: A Practical Manual:* Dodd, Mead & Company New York 1895

Leonard, Terri, *In the Women's Clubhouse: The Greatest Women Golfers in Their Own Words:* Contemporary Books Chicago 2000

Lewis, Catherine M., *Considerable Passions: Golf, The Masters, and the Legacy of Bobby Jones:* Triumph Books (Chicago) & The Atlanta Historical Society Atlanta 2000

Lewis, Peter N., *The Dawn of Professional Golf 1894-1914:* Hobbs & McEwan, New Ridley, Northumberland 1995

Lewis, Peter N. and Howe, Angela D., *The Golfers: The Story Behind the Painting:* National Galleries of Scotland Edinburgh 2004

Livingston III, Ralph S., *Thomas Steward Jr.: Golf Cleek and Iron Maker St. Andrews, Scotland:* Gibson Graphics United States 2010

Londino, Lawrence J., *Tiger Woods: A Biography:* Greenwood Publishing Westport, Connecticut 2006

Love III, Davis, *Every Shot I Take: Lessons Learned About Golf, Life, and a Father's Love:* Simon & Schuster New York 1997

Low, George, with Barkow, Al, *The Master of Puttig:* Atheneum New York 1983

Lowe, Stephen R., *Sir Walter and Mr. Jones: Walter Hagen, Bobby Jones, and the Rise of American Golf:* Sleeping Bear Press Chelsea, Michigan 2000

Lucas, Laddie, *The Sport of Prince's: Reflections of a Golfer:* Stanley Paul London 1980

Luedtke, Eleanor, *In Good Company: A Centennial History of The Country Club of Detroit 1897-1997:* Country Club of Detroit 1997

M

Macdonald, Charles Blair, *Scotland's Gift: Golf – Reminiscences:* Charles Scribner's Sons New York 1928

McCord, Robert, *Golf Book of Days: Fascinating Facts and Stories For Every Day of the Year:* Citadel Press New York 1995, 2002

McGimpsey, K.W., *The Story of the Golf Ball:* Philip Wilson Publishers London 2003

MacKenzie, Alister, *The Spirit of St. Andrews:* Sleeping Bear Press Chelsea, Michigan 1995

Mackenzie, Richard, *A Wee Nip at the 19th Hole:* Sleeping Bear Press, Chelsea, Michigan 1997

Mackie, Keith, *Golf At St Andrews:* Pelican Publishing Gretna, Louisiana 1995

Mackie, Keith, *Open Championship Courses of Britain:* Pelican Publishing Gretna, Louisiana 1997

Maddex, Diane, *The Breakers: A Century of Grand Traditions:* The Breakers Palm Beach Palm Beach 2004

Malcolm, David and Crabtree, Peter E., *Tom Morris of St. Andews: The Colossus of Golf 1821-1908;* Birlinn Limited Edinburgh 2010

Mahoney, Jack, *The Golf History of New England: Centennial Edition:* Jack Mahoney Weston, Massachusetts 1995

Mallon, Bill and Jerris, Rand, *The Historical Dictionary of Golf:* Scarecrow Press Lanham, Maryland 2011

Marshall, Stuart, *St Andrews and Its Golfing Legends:* Tempus Publishing Limited Stroud, Gloucestershire 2000

Martin, H.B., *Fifty Years of American Golf:* Dodd, Mead & Company New York 1936

Martin, John Stuart, *The Curious History of the Golf Ball: Mankind's Most Fascinating Sphere:* Horizon Press New York 1968

Martin, J. Peter, *Craig Wood: The Blond Bomber Native Son of Lake Placid:* Adirondack Golf Lake Placid 2002

Mathison, Thomas, *The Goff: An Heroi-Comical Poem in Three Cantos:* Scotland 1743

Matthew, Sidney L., *Wry Stories on The Road Hole:* Sleeping Bear Press Chelsea, Michigan 2000

Matthew, Sidney L., *Kiltie the Kingmaker: The Ten Lost Lessons of Bobby Jones's Teacher Stewart Maiden:* Sports Media Group Ann Arbor, Michigan 2004

Matthew, Sidney L., *The History of Bobby Jones' Clubs:* The Impregnable Quadrilateral Press Tallahassee 1992

McDaniel, Pete, *Uneven Lies: The Heroic Story of African-Americans in Golf:* The American Golfer Greenwich, Connecticut 2000

McCormach, Mark H., *Arnie: The Evolution of a Legend:* Simon & Schuster New York 1967

McDonald, Mark A. and Milne, George R., *Cases in Sports Marketing:* Jones and Bartlett Publishers Sudbury, Massachusetts 1999

McNew, Monte, *Golf In The Ozarks,* Arcadia Press Charleston 2006

Merrins, Eddie with Mike Purkey, *Playing A Round With The Little Pro: A Life in the Game:* Atria Books / Simon & Schuster New York 2006

Michaels, Al, with Wertheim, L. Jon, *You Can't Make This Up: Miracles, Memories, and the Perfect Marriage of Sports and Television:* William Morrow New York 2014

Michelson, Richard, *Twice as Good: The Story of William Powell and Clearview, The Only Golf Course Designed, Built, and Owned by an African American:* Sleeping Bear Press Chelsea, Michigan 2014

Miller, Eleanora Foulis, *Saftest O'The Family:* Self-published 1995

Miller, Jeff, *Grown at Glen Garden: Ben Hogan, Byron Nelson, and the Little Texas Course That Propelled Them to Stardom:* Skyhorse Publishing New York 2012

Mishler, Jack L., *Robert Simpson: Carnoustie:* JLM Golf Fountain Hills, Arizona 2001

Moorhead, Richard and Wynne, Nick, *Golf In Florida 1886-1950:* Arcadia Publishing Charleston 2008

Moreton, John F., *A Century of Golf at Huntercombe:* Grant Books Worcestershire 2001

Morrison, Ian, *The Pictorial History of Golf:* Bison Books London 1990

Moss, Richard J., *The Kingdom of Golf in America:* University of Nebraska Press Lincoln 2013

Moss, Richard J., *Golf ad the American Country Club:* University of Illinois Press Urbana 2001

Murdoch, Joseph S.F., *The Library of Golf:* Gale Research Company Detroit 1968

N

Nelson, Byron, *The Little Black Book: The Personal Diary of Golf Legend Byron Nelson 1935-1947:* The Summit Publishing Group Arlington, Texas 1995

Nelson, Byron, *Winning Golf:* A.S. Barnes New York 1946

Nelson, Byron, *The Byron Nelson Story:* The Old Golf Shop Cincinnati 1980

Nosner, Ellen Susanna, *Clearview: America's Course:* Foxsong Haslett, Michigan 2000

O

Oakley Country Club, *Oakley Country Club 1898-1973:* Oakley Country Club Watertown, Massachusetts 1973

Ouimet, Francis, *A Game of Golf: A Book of Reminiscence:* Riverside Press Cambridge, Massachusetts 1932

Owen, David, *The Chosen One: Tiger Woods and the Dilemma of Greatness:* Simon & Schuster New York 2001

Owen, David, *The Making of the Masters: Clifford Roberts, Augusta National, and Golf's Most Prestigious Tournament:* Simon & Schuster New York 1999

P

Pace, Lee, *Padge: Pinehurst's Coach, Storyteller and Friend:* The Pilot Southern Pines 2003

Pace, Lee, et al, *The Spirit of Pinehurst:* Pinehurst Pinehurst 2004

Park Junior, Willie, *The Art of Putting:* J.J. Gray & Company Edinburgh 1920

Park Junior, Willie, *The Game of Golf: Champion Golfer 1887-1889:* Longmans, Green, and Company London 1896

Patmont, Robert E. with earlier narrative of Barnett, Frank H., *The History of Claremont Country Club:* Claremont Country Club Oakland, California 1988

Peek, Walter A., *Seventy Years at Wykagyl: 1898-1968:* The Wykagyl Golf Club Pelham, New York 1968

Peper, George, *Shinnecock Hills Golf Club: 1891-1991:* Shinnecock Hills Golf Club 1991

Peper, George, with Tiegreen, Mary, *The Secret of Golf: A Century of Groundbreaking, Innovative, and Occasionally Outlandish Ways to Master the World's Most Vexing Game:* Workman Publishing New York 2005

Peper, George, *The Story of Golf:* TV Books New York 1999

Pioppi, Anthony, *To The Nines:* Sports Media Group Ann Arbor 2006

Platt, Simon, *Centenary: 100 Years of Turnberry:* Turnberry Scotland 2006

PGA of America, *The Book of Golf: 1951 Ryder Cup Matches:* PGA of America Chicago 1951

PGA TOUR, *Ben Hogan Tour Information:* PGA Tour Ponte Vedra Beach, Florida 1989

Price, Charles, and Rogers, Jr. George C., *The Carolina Lowcountry: Birthplace of American Golf 1786:* Sea Pines Company Hilton Head 1980

Q

Quirin, William, *America's Linksland: A Century of Long Island Golf:* Sleeping Bear Press Chelsea, Michigan 2002

Quirin, Dr. William L., *Golf Club of the MGA; A Centennial Hisotro of Golf in the New York Metropolitan Area:* Golf Magazine Properties New York 1997

Quirin, William L, *The Ridgewood Country Club: Celebrating a Century of Golf 1890-1990:* Sammis Publishing 1990

R

Rapoport, Ron, *The Immortal Bobby: Bobby Jones and the Golden Age of Golf:* John Wiley & Sons New York 2005

Revolta, Johnny and Cleveland, Charles B., *Johnny Revolta's Short Cuts to Better Golf:* Thomas Y. Crowell Company New York 1949

Richardson, Forrest L. and Fine, Mark K., *Bunkers, Pits & Other Hazards: A Guide to the Design, Maintenance & Preservation of Golf's Essential Elements:* John Wiley & Sons Hoboken 2006

Roberts, Clifford, *The Story of the Augusta National Golf Club:* Double Day & Company Garden City, New York 1976

Royal Montreal Golf Club, *The Royal Montreal Golf Club 1873-1973: the Centennial of Golf in North America:* Royal Montreal Golf Club Montreal 1973

Royal & Ancient Golf Club of St. Andrews, *Decisions By The Rules of Golf Committee of The Royal & Ancient Golf Club of St. Andrews 1909-1928:* W.C. Henderson & Son, LTD University Press of St. Andrews 1929

S

Salem Press, The Editors of, *Great Athletes: Golf & Tennis:* Salem Press Pasadena 2010

Sampson, Curt, *The Masters: Golf, Money, and Power in Augusta, Georgia:* Villard Books New York 1998

Sampson, Curt, *The Slam: Bobby Jones and the Price of Glory:* Rodale Emmaus, Pennsylvania 2005

Sanson, Nanette S. et al, *Champions of Women's Golf: Celebrating Fifty Years of the LPGA:* Quailmark Books Naples, Florida 2000

Sarazen, Gene, *Thirty Year of Championship Golf: The Life and Times of Gene Sarazen:* Prentice-Hall New York 1950

Schupak, Adam, *Deane Beman: Golf Driving Force:* East Cottage Press Orlando 2011

Scott, Tom, *The Concise Dictionary of Golf:* Mayflower Books New York 1978

Seelig, Pat, *Historic Golf Courses of America:* Taylor Publishing Dallas 1994

Shackelford, Geoff, *The Captain: George C. Thomas Jr. and his Golf Architecture:* Captain Fantastic Publishing Santa Monica 1996

Shackelford, Geoff, *The Golf Age of Golf Design:* Sleeping Bear Press Chelsea, Michigan 1999

Shapiro, Elizabeth W. Pippitt, et al, *Golf Has Never Failed Me: The Lost Commentaries of Legendary Golf Architect Donald J. Ross:* Sleeping Bear Press Chelsea, Michigan 1996

Shapiro, Mel, *Golf: A Turn-of-the-Century Treasury:* Castle Secaucus, New Jersey 1986

Shea, Dr. Daniel, *Oakley Country Club: The First 100 Years 1898-1998 A Special Legacy:* Oakley Country Club Watertown, Massachusetts 1998

Sheehan, Laurence, *A Commonwealth of Golfers 1903-2003:* Massachusetts Golf Association Norton, Massachusetts 2002

Shefchik, Rick, *From Fields to Fairways: Classic Golf Clubs of Minnesota:* University of Minnesota Press Minneapolis 2012

Shelley, Jeff, and Riste, Michael, *Championships & Friendships: The First 100 Years of the Pacific Northwest Golf Association:* Pacific Northwest Golf Association Seattle 1999

Sherman, Adam, *Golf's Book of Firsts:* Courage Press Philadelphia 2002

Simpson, W.G., *The Art of Golf:* David Douglas Edinburgh 1887 USGA Facsimile 1982

Sinnette, Calvin H., *Forbidden Fairways: African Americas and the Game of Golf:* Sleeping Bear Press Chelsea, Michigan 1998

Smith, Douglas LaRue, *Winged Foot Story: The Golf, The People, The Friendly Trees:* Winged Foot Golf Club Mamaroneck, New York 1994

Smith, Marilynn with Cayne, Bob, *Have Clubs, Will Travel:* Ambassador Publishing Goodyear, Arizona 2012

Sommers, Robert, *The U.S. Open: Golf's Ultimate Challenge:* Atheneum New York 1987

Sounes, Howard, *The Wicked Game: Arnold Palmer, Jack Nicklaus, Tiger Woods, and the Story of Modern Golf:* William Morrow New York 2004

Steel, Donald and Lewis, Peter N., *Traditions & Change: The Royal & Ancient Golf Club 1939-2004 Volume 3:* Grant Books Worcestershire 2004

Steinbreder, John, *Club Life: The Game Golfers Play:* Taylor Trade Publishing Lanham, Maryland 2006

Steinbreder, John, *Golf Kohler: In the New and Old Worlds:* Kohler Company Kohler Wisconsin 2010

Stephen, Walter, *Willie Park Junior: The Man who took Golf to the World:* Lauth Press Limited Edinburgh 2005

Stirk, David L., *Carry Your Bag, Sir?: The Story of Golf's Caddies:* H.F. & G. Witherby LTD London 1989

Stirk, David, *Golf: The Great Clubmakers:* H.F.&G. Witherby Ltd, London 1991

Stirk, David, *Golf: History and Tradition 1500-1945:* Excellent Press Ludlow 1998

Stirk, David, *Golf: The History of an Obsession:* Phaidon Press Limited Oxford 1987

Strege, John, *When War Played Through: Golf During World War II:* Gotham Books New York 2005

Straus, Frank, and Dunnigan, Brian Leigh, *Walk a Crooked Trail: A Centennial History of Wawashkamo Golf Club:* Wawashkamo Golf Club Mackinac Island 2000

Stricklin, Art, *Links, Lore, & Legends: The Story of Texas Golf:* Taylor Trade Publishing, Lanham, Maryland 2005

Sumner, Tracy, *Karsten's Way,* Northfield Publishing Chicago 2000

T

Taylor, Dawson, *The Masters: All About Its History, Its Records, Its Players, Its Remarkable Course and Even More Remarkable Tournament:* A.S Barnes and Company New York 1973

Taylor, J.H., *Taylor On Golf: Impressions, Comments, and Hints:* Hutchinson & Co. London 1902

Tolhurst, Desmond, *Golf at Marion:* Marion Golf Club Ardmore 1989

Tolhurst, Desmond, *St. Andrew's Golf Club: The Birthplace of American Golf:* Karjan Publishing Rye Brook, New York 1989

Trebus, Robert S. and Wolffe Jr., Richard C., *Baltusrol 100 Years: The Centennial History of Baltusrol Golf Club:* Baltusrol Golf Club New Jersey 1995

Trimble, Frances G., *One Hundred Years of Champions and Change: The History of Austin Country Club:* Whitley Company Austin 1999

Tufts, Richard S., *The Principles Behind The Rules of Golf:* Pinehurst Publishers Pinehurst 1961

Tufts, Richard S., *The Scottish Invasion:* Pinehurst Publishers Pinehurst 1962

Tulloch, W.W., *The Life of Tom Morris: With Glimpses of St Andrews and It's Golfing Celebrities:* T. Lerner Laurie London 1908

U

Unknown, *A Pictorial History of American Golf:* Willow Creek Press Minocqua, Wisconsin 1998

United States Golf Association, *Golf The Greatest Game: The USGA Celebrates Golf in America:* Harper Collins Publishers New York 1994

United States Golf Association, *Golf's Golden Age:* National Geographic Washington D.C. 2005

V

Vardon, Harry, *How to Play Golf:* George W. Jacobs & Co. Philadelphia 1912

Vold, Mona, *Different Strokes: The Lives and Teaching of the Game's Wisest Women:* Simon & Schuster New York 1999

W

Whalin, George, *Retail Superstars: Inside the 25 Best Independent Stores in America:* Portfolio Books Ltd. 2009

Wegener, Parr J., *Keep the Ball a Rolling: A Pictorial History of Claremont Country Club 1903-2003:* The Donning Company Virginia Beach 2003

Weiser, Marjorie P.K. and Arbeiter, Jean S., *Womanlist:* Atheneum New York 1981

Wethered, H.N., and Simpson, T., *Design For Golf:* The Sportsman's Book Club Norwich 1952

Whigham, H.J. *How To Play Golf:* Herbert S. Stone & Company Chicago 1900

William, Michael, *History of Golf:* Chartwell Books Secaucus, New Jersey 1987

Wilson, Mark, *The Golf Club Identification & Price Guide III: '50 To '93:* Ralph Maltby Enterprises Newark, Ohio 1993

Wind, Herbert Warren, *The Complete Golfer:* Simon & Schuster New York 1954

Wind, Herbert Warren, *The Story of American Golf:* Murray Printing Company Wakefield, Massachusetts 1948, 1956

Wright, Ben with Shiels, Michael Patrick, *Good Bounces & Bad Lies: The Autobiography of Ben Wright:* Sleeping Bear Press Chelsea, Michigan, 1999

Z

Zuckerman, Joel, *Pete Dye Golf Courses: Fifty Years of Visionary Design:* Abrams New York 2008

Articles & Periodicals

American Golfer Magazine (1908-1923)

Appleton Post Crescent, Appleton, Wisconsin

Golf Illustrated Magazine (1914-1934)

Golf Magazine

Golfweek Magazine

Golf World Magazine

Golfdom Magazine

Hong Kong Golfer Magazine

NewspaperArchives.com

New York Times Archives

Oshkosh Daily Northwestern, Oshkosh, Wisconsin

PGA Magazine

PGA TOUR Media Guides

Slate Magazine

Sports Illustrated Magazine

The Golfer (1895-1903)

Time Magazine

U.S.G.A. Magazine

Interviews

Bare, Mary Lamprey, *Great-granddaughter of Willie & Georgina Campbell*, Center Harbor, New Hampshire, October 3, 2011

Borocz, Matthew, *President's Cup Room, TPC Sawgrass*, Ponte Vedra Beach, Florida, April 3, 2015

Borocz, Jennifer Heinz, *President's Cup Room, TPC Sawgrass,* Ponte Vedra Beach, Florida, April 3, 2015

Burgess, Charles D., *Grandson of Chay Burgess – Francis Ouimet's Teacher*, Boston, Massachusetts, October 5, 2011

Davison, Peter S., Ponte Vedra Beach, Florida, June 2011

De la Torre, Manuel, *Milwaukee Country Club,* River Hills, Wisconsin, July 2011

Dettlaff, Gordon, *Interview on Hank Dettlaff and Johnny Revolta,* Centralia, Washington, November 7, 2011

Hartjen, Jodee, *Granddaughter of Chester Horton, The Horton Brothers*, Park Ridge, Illinois, July 23, 2011

Jemsek, Frank, *Interview on his father Joe Jemsek,* Coghill Golf Club, Lemont, Illinois, July 24, 2011

LaBauve, Sandy Lumpkin, *Sea Island Resort,* Sea Island, Georgia, December 31, 2013

Lamprey, Steward, *Grandson of Willie & Georgina Campbell*, Center Harbor, New Hampshire, October 3, 2011

Lumpkin, Jack, *Sea Island Resort,* Sea Island, Georgia, December 31, 2013

Mahoney, Honorable Judge Patrick, *Phone interview on his father Pat Mahoney and Karsten Solheim,* San Francisco, California, August 20, 2014

Morton, Ken (Senior), *Haggin Oaks Golf Complex,* Sacramento, California, November 9, 2011

Morton, Ken (Junior), *Haggin Oaks Golf Complex,* Sacramento, California, November 9, 2011

O'Connor, Jennifer Webster, *Prouts Neck Country Club,* Scarborough, Maine, October 4, 2011

O'Mara, Jim, *Charles River Country Club,* Newton Centre, Massachusetts, October 5, 2011

Nienhaus, Mary Beth, *Phone Interview,* Appleton, Wisconsin, April 2015

Nye, Bob, *Wooster Country Club*, Wooster, Ohio, October 2, 2012

Nye, Grey, *Penn State University,* State College, Pennsylvania, March 27, 2012

Padgett, Donald II, *Pinehurst Resort,* Pinehurst, North Carolina, June 24, 2011

Turnesa, Joe Junior, *Multiple phone interviews on his father and the Turnesa family,* Sarasota, Florida, Spring 2015

Walsh, Brendan, *The Country Club – Brookline,* Brookline, Massachusetts, October 5, 2011

Welshans, Gary, *Wooster Country Club,* Wooster, Ohio, October 2, 2012

Museums & Archives

Center for History – Wheaton, Illinois – Alberta Adamson, President & CEO

Clemson University Tiger Prints, Clemson, South Carolina – David Hueber Dissertation

Michigan State University Libraries – The Turfgrass Information Center

Oshkosh Public Library, Oshkosh, Wisconsin

Oshkosh Public Museum, Oshkosh, Wisconsin

PGA of America Document and Photography Archive

PGA Museum of Golf – Probst Library

PGA Museum of Golf – Port St. Lucie, Florida

The Tufts Archives – Pinehurst, North Carolina

USGA Museum & Arnold Palmer Center for Golf History, Far Hills, New Jersey

USGA Research Center, Far Hills, New Jersey – Nancy Stulack, Librarian

USGA Seagle Electronic Golf Library

World Golf Hall of Fame, St. Augustine, Florida

ACKNOWLEDGEMENTS

The text for *PGA Centennial: Celebrating the History of the Golf Professional*, the official PGA centennial commemorative, is used with the permission of Billy Dettlaff, PGA Master Professional #58, whose seven-plus years of in-depth research and writing on the game and the golf profession represents what is believed to be the most detailed study on the subject in the Library of Golf. The text presented herein represents approximately ten percent of the full manuscript, which is scheduled to be published in the latter half of 2016 under the title *Doctors of the Game: Honoring the Past - Inspiring the Future*. For more information about this comprehensive volume, including release date and purchase options, please visit:

DoctorsOfTheGame.com

BillyDettlaff.com

PGA OF AMERICA

Dan Baker, PGA
Sr. Director, Partnership Development

Bob Denney
PGA Historian

Larry Heymont
Deputy, Chief Executive Staff

SKYBOX PRESS

Peter Gotfredson
Publisher

Nate Beale/SeeSullivan
Designer

The BookDesigners
Cover Design

Porter Binks
Photo Editor

Mikayla Butchart
Copyeditor

Scott Gummer
Editor

Lisa Segraves
Project Coordinator

Swen Gummer
Project Intern

BarnacleMediaSD
Social Media

Billy Dettlaff, PGA
Author

John Steinbreder
Editor

The PGA of America offers special thanks to all of the Members and Staff who made significant contributions, including Craig Dolch, PGA and Tom Galvin, PGA. Additionally, the PGA of America would like to thank Mike McGee, Montana Pritchard Photography, and Scott Tolley.

Skybox Press thanks Patrick Sommers; Pete Bevacqua, Jeff Price, Wendy Akner, Joni Lockridge, Nick Pepe, and Kelly Elbin; Dean James, Mike Jonas, Mark Quintel, Laird Small, PGA, and Mickey Leuenberger.

Billy Dettlaff wishes to thank Wally Uihlein, Peter Broome, Brentan Vivian, Helen Atter, Debbie Foley, and his wife Geraldine Dettlaff. He dedicates his research to his parents, Henry & Helen Dettlaff, who inspired his career as a PGA Professional.

John Steinbreder would like to thank Joe Gomes, Jim Nugent, and Cynthia Crolius.

www.skyboxpress.com
info@skyboxpress.com
(888) 527-5556

ISBN: 978-0-9906671-5-5

Manufactured in Malaysia

9 8 7 6 5 4 3 2 1

Published by Skybox Press, an imprint of Luxury Custom Publishing, LLC.